A Good Death:

A Practical Guide to Maintaining Control of your End-of-Life Journey

C. Susan Cass RN, FNP

BALBOA.
PRESS

A DIVISION OF HAY HOUSE

Balboa Press books may be ordered through booksellers or by contacting:

Balboa Press
A Division of Hay House
1663 Liberty Drive
Bloomington, IN 47403
www.balboapress.com
1 (877) 407-4847

Because of the dynamic nature of the Internet, any web addresses or links contained in this book may have changed since publication and may no longer be valid. The views expressed in this work are solely those of the author and do not necessarily reflect the views of the publisher, and the publisher hereby disclaims any responsibility for them.

The information contained in this book is not intended to be a substitute for professional legal advice. The author encourages you to seek legal advice when necessary. Names and other identifying information have been changed to protect the identity of patients and their families.

Any people depicted in stock imagery provided by Thinkstock are models, and such images are being used for illustrative purposes only. Certain stock imagery © Thinkstock.

Print information available on the last page.

ISBN: 978-1-5043-3048-0 (sc)
ISBN: 978-1-5043-3050-3 (hc)
ISBN: 978-1-5043-3049-7 (e)

Library of Congress Control Number: 2015904914

Balboa Press rev. date: 4/28/2015

To my mother Mary Lou Cass, RN extraordinaire,
my inspiration, my compass.

CONTENTS

CHAPTER 1

INTRODUCTION

Everyone dies, but no one is dead.
—Tibetan saying

I have worked in various capacities in the healthcare field for over thirty-five years. These professional experiences, coupled with my own personal experiences, have given me intimate knowledge of the hardships of illness, aging, and frailty, as well as firsthand experience observing family interactions and dynamics when a loved one is ill and reaches the final stages of his or her mortal life.

Initially, I worked as a nurse's aide (now called a patient-care tech) in a nursing home (now called a long-term care facility). The residents (formerly called patients) of the nursing home ranged from people who were self-sufficient and had minimal needs to those who were completely dependent on the staff for all their basic needs, including feeding, bathing, and all bodily functions.

Just as there was a wide range of resident needs, there was a wide range of family involvement in the resident's life and care. The response by families to a loved one's illness and frailty varied greatly. Reactions ranged from complete denial of the patient's condition and non-involvement, where the family ignores the patient completely and refuses to acknowledge they are ill, to

1

the opposite extreme, where the family is over-involved. An over-involved family will try to dictate every minute of the patient's life and run roughshod over the patient, taking away the patient's right to make decisions, telling the patient what he or she will or will not do in the belief that the family knows best. Families that cannot accept the patient's illness and that abandon the person at this crucial time cause extreme emotional pain to the patient. This abandonment often leads to the patient being placed in a long-term care facility. I think this is a sad situation; it stems from selfishness or poor coping skills on the part of the family, since they are unable or unwilling to "walk in the shoes" of the patient and put their own needs aside in order to help their loved one.

These early years working in the nursing home laid the foundation for how I have interacted with patients and families throughout my career. I have always remembered those I cared for at the nursing home. The residents taught me to be truthful with them, to respect them (after all, they had had rich life experiences that I as a young person could learn from), and to always remember that even though they may suffer from severe dementia, were nonverbal, or were bedridden, they were still someone's mother, father, sister, brother, aunt, uncle, child, or loved one.

I grew up in a small rural community, and working in the nursing home brought me very close to the experience of death and dying. My mother is a registered nurse (RN), and she would often talk about patients she had cared for. She knew almost everyone in our small town and had taken care of many of them over the years. Hearing about her work experiences taught me at an early age that everyone dies eventually, but her job was to take care of them to the best of her ability and to keep them as comfortable as possible.

While I was working at the nursing home, many residents died, as would be expected, given their advanced age and multiple chronic illnesses. This is something I expected when working with the frail elderly. I remember one winter when fatalities were particularly high. Every week, at least one resident died, and sometimes several died in a single week. I read *On Death and Dying* by Dr. Elisabeth Kübler-Ross because I wanted to know what those who were dying were experiencing. I also wanted to know if there was something I could do to help make their transition more comfortable. The book helped me to understand that dying is the natural progression of life, that it should not be faced alone, and that we all will face our own death. How we face that death and how others help us are paramount to having a good death.

I also learned from the residents that death was not something to avoid or fear. I noticed that they never seemed upset or scared when they spoke of dying. It was a topic that was discussed with pragmatism. Over the years I have had many patients tell me they are tired of living and look forward to what lies ahead for them. People who live with a severe illness or multiple prolonged chronic diseases may find the challenges of living insurmountable and become fatigued with living. The oldest old, those eighty-five years and older, may feel they have lived so long that they have outlived their usefulness. This can be hard for family members to understand. My father, who died at the age of ninety-two, would speak of how he had lived too long. All his friends had died. It saddened him that none of his friends would be able to attend his funeral, for they had all preceded him in death. In the last two years of his life my father developed dementia. He became aware of his declining mental capacity and was terribly upset by this. He would often wish for death to take him and spare him the degradation of his mind. He would ask me to help him die before the dementia completely took him over. This was terribly painful to watch as my father become completely dependent on others for his care. It was especially painful because I knew he was

3

miserable. By the time my father died, he could only remember our dog, and seeing her was the only thing that gave him pleasure. He had forgotten everyone else, although he did say he thought we were nice people.

The residents of the nursing home seemed to have an awareness of when they would die. Oftentimes at the end of my shift, I would say "I'll see you tomorrow," and sometimes they would respond with "I won't be here" or "no you won't." At first, in my youth and naïveté, I dismissed these statements. How could they possibly know that? At first I was surprised to find that they were not there when I returned, just as they said. They had died. But as time passed and this occurred repeatedly, I knew that they really did know something I couldn't know. What stayed with me the most was not the fact that they died but that those words were always accompanied by a calm demeanor and often a slight smile on the lips that told me they were at peace with their life and they were ready for whatever came next. I found this comforting. To have an awareness of when their life on earth would end seemed to provide some comfort and even control to the residents. They never appeared to be upset, but rather they were holding a secret that I was fortunate to have them share with me. Based on these experiences, I have never considered that dying might be scary or something to be avoided, but rather another chapter of living. I learned that grieving is for those left behind, not for the one who has died. They are now at their final resting place, and those remaining must continue on without them. This can be a difficult and daunting task.

After I left the nursing home and went to nursing school, my responsibilities changed. I no longer worked in a nursing home filled with elderly people, where expectations were focused not on curing an acute disease but instead on managing chronic diseases or illnesses. Now I worked in the acute care setting, a hospital which had an entirely different focus—a focus on combating every disease, whether acute or chronic, to the most extreme degree possible. Working in the hospital, I was surrounded by the daily hope for a cure and the daily denial that death was inevitable. Death was the enemy and needed to be conquered at all costs, regardless of the futility of our actions or the pain we inflicted on the patients in the course of treating them. This led to patients being subjected to multiple painful and futile treatments, often without their full and informed consent.

It was not unusual for family members to ask the healthcare team to withhold information from the patient regarding their diagnosis or prognosis for fear that, if they knew the truth, they would "give up." Physicians, families, and nurses were only too happy to withhold such important information, not out of malice, but rather out of concern. They thought they were doing the patient a favor by not being truthful. The prevailing thought was that patients shouldn't know how sick they really were, as this would negatively impact their will to survive and to carry on. They would "give up." Families routinely withheld information about the patient's prognosis and often gave the patient false hope for recovery. This was quite a common practice across the United States in the 1970s and 1980s. At this time rapid innovations were taking place in healthcare, including new medications, surgical techniques, and other technologies such as dialysis and mechanical ventilation. These were used with gusto, and there was a general feeling that we could treat any malady. The topic of death and dying was taboo. The death of a patient was viewed as a failure— that we didn't try hard enough or long enough to save them.

I understand now that this was an approach that not only gave false hope but also subjected patients to treatments they may not have wanted had they known the truth regarding their illness and had they been given the option of making their own decisions. It also denied patients and their families the opportunity to come to terms with a terminal diagnosis and allow them to participate in decisions regarding end-of-life care. It also denied patients the time to get their affairs in order and possibly address unresolved issues prior to dying.

Although it is a difficult subject for many people (including healthcare providers) to discuss, I believe we need to foster an environment where there can be open and honest conversations among families, significant others, physicians, nurses, and clergy regarding treatment options and end-of-life care. We need an environment where we can encourage patients to become fully engaged in their care if they wish and where we ensure that they are in control of their own destiny and that others are not doing to them what they *think* patients may want or what they think is best for them. Even today in 2015 we continue to give patients and their families false hope and encourage them to submit to procedures, surgeries, and treatments by emphasizing the potential benefits, while minimizing the potential side effects or harm that may occur as a result of the treatment. False hope continues to be the number-one prescription for those with terminal diseases.

To this end, I have written this book to help answer questions anyone may face who is diagnosed with a terminal illness or who may be engaged in end-of-life decisions either for themselves or for someone close to them. It is intended to help them understand the options for managing end-of-life care, whether this means undergoing extensive treatment, withdrawal of treatment, refusal or withholding of treatment, palliative care, or hospice care.

Chapter 2

History of Caring for the Ill in the United States

Without health life is not life; it is only a state of languor and suffering - an image of death.
—Buddha

Since the beginning of time humans have struggled with disease and death; the inevitability of death has long been difficult to accept. From the earliest accounts man has searched for that which will make him live longer. Herodotus, a Greek historian who lived in the fifth century B.C., mentioned a fountain containing a special kind of water in the land of the Macrobians, which gave them exceptional longevity. In 1513 Ponce de León searched for the fountain of youth in what is now Florida. Of course there isn't a fountain of youth, but with the explosion in medical advances, which includes vaccinations, new surgical techniques, medications, chemotherapy, radiation therapy, CPR, mechanical ventilation, antibiotics, antiviral agents, and improved diagnostic imaging such as the CT scan, PET scan and MRI, people are living longer and the expectation for a cure is always high.

Although medical advances are important and we look to these to treat our illnesses, we also need to remember that nutrition, exercise, education, and public safety are more important in determining longevity.

Prior to World War II the cost of hospitalization and healthcare was primarily the responsibility of the patient or family. Very few people had health insurance. Most individuals were cared for and died in the home, surrounded by family and friends. The family was the natural locus of most of the care of the sick, with the women of the family providing most of that care.[1] When someone died, family members prepared the body for burial.

During World War II women entered the workforce at an unprecedented rate, which removed them from the home and made it impossible for them to provide in-home care the way they had previously. After the war women continued to work outside the home, and extended family members were not available to care for and support the ill and dying.[2] More hospitals were being built, and they were easily accessible for the family to visit. Hospitals were originally structured to take care of people who did not have family to care for them. However, this has changed. Hospitals were initially built mostly in ports or river towns such as Philadelphia, New York, Boston, New Orleans, and Louisville—centers of commerce where strangers were likely to be stranded sick or where people were likely to be found working and living alone.[3] The increase in hospital beds encouraged the ill to be cared for in the hospital rather than in the home. In 1949 49.5 percent of deaths in the United States occurred in institutions, by 1958 that number had increased to 60.9 percent, and today 75 percent of Americans will die in institutions.[4]

Private group insurance was introduced in 1929, and employer-based insurance became common during World War II when wage freezes prompted employers to introduce other benefits as a way of attracting workers. The passage of the Medicare and Medicaid act in 1965 provided insurance for those aged sixty-five and older and for those with disabilities, increasing the general availability of insurance and intensifying the number of encounters with the healthcare system and the use of technology.[5] When a person has health insurance, they are more likely to be offered and consent to procedures or treatments and to be hospitalized since there is no financial risk to them.[6] With the movement of care of the dying to institutions, the care of the patient shifted from the women and family to physicians, nurses, funeral directors, and chaplains.[7] This shift changed the dynamic of dying from involvement of the family to removal of the family as the patient's caregiver and made possible denial of a terminal illness by the family and patient. It also allowed an avoidance of talking about the illness and interacting with the dying. The dying became isolated in their experience. This isolation was extended by the physicians and nurses caring for the patient, as the topic of dying was avoided.

At this time it was common practice to withhold information about the diagnosis and prognosis from patients due to the concern that patients were not able to handle the truth. There was a mistaken notion that patients would "give up" if they were told their diagnosis and prognosis. This withholding of information caused further isolation of the patient. My own family offers an example. When I was young, my aunt Lila was in the hospital, and the physician initially thought she had cancer. Although the diagnosis proved incorrect and she recovered, the family, including my mother who is an RN, asked the physician to withhold this information from my aunt because they thought it would upset her too much. Later my aunt found out about this deception and was terribly angry that we hadn't been truthful with her. She said she wanted to be able to deal with her illness regardless of what that illness might be.

When patients are not informed about their diagnosis and prognosis, they are robbed of the opportunity to make their own decisions and maintain control over their medical care, which may include end-of-life decisions. Uninformed patients are not given the opportunity to put their affairs in order or to spend time with their family and friends.

Family relationships often become strained when someone is facing an incurable illness. Being truthful with patients gives them the opportunity to resolve interpersonal conflicts, and it gives the family the opportunity to emotionally support and spend time with the patient, as well as address their own emotional needs.

Life expectancy has steadily increased over the centuries. In 1776 when the country was founded, life expectancy was thirty-five years. In 1950 life expectancy increased to 68 (which is why retirement and Social Security benefits were set to start at age 65). In 2011 life expectancy increased further to 76.3 years for males and 81.1 years for females.[8] Over 70 million Americans will reach age 65 by 2030. The number of people living into their 90s and 100s is also increasing. The "oldest old" (those 85 years and older) is the most rapidly increasing age group.[9] The number of elderly African-Americans over 65 is expected to reach 10.4 million by 2050. Morbidity and mortality rates are higher among older African-American adults than any other racial and ethnic group. Leading causes of death for African Americans aged 65 and older are heart disease, cancer, stroke, diabetes, and pneumonia.[10]

From the 1700s to the 1900s the majority of deaths were sudden and followed a short illness. Today most deaths are slow. The age at which someone dies has also changed. In 1900 it was common for a family to have buried at least one child; fifty-three percent of all deaths were among children under the age of 15. People over the age of 65 only accounted for 17 percent of deaths. In the nineteenth century the leading causes of death were infections such as pneumonia, influenza, and cholera. The development of antibiotics and vaccines, along with improvements in nutrition and sanitation, including clean water supplies, improved transportation systems, exercise, education, and workplace safety, led to a dramatic increase in life expectancy. By the end of the 1960s people over the age of 65 accounted for 67 percent of deaths, and in 2011 they accounted for 72 percent of all deaths, totaling 1.8 million deaths per year.[11]

The most common cause of death has shifted from acute illness to chronic diseases, which may occur over years or even decades of a person's life. Approximately half of American adults have been diagnosed with at least one chronic disease. Chronic diseases such as hypertension (high blood pressure), heart disease, diabetes, and Alzheimer's dementia are common and increasing. Seven out of ten deaths among Americans each year are from chronic diseases such as heart disease, heart failure, liver failure, COPD, Alzheimer's dementia, diabetes, stroke, and others.[12] Today 10 percent of Americans suffer from type 2 diabetes, and 32 percent have hypertension. Five million older adults suffer from Alzheimer's dementia, and that number is expected to increase to 16 million by 2050.[13] In 2011, the leading cause of death in the United States was chronic heart disease, followed by cancer. Heart disease and cancer accounted for 47 percent of all deaths.[14]

The advancement of technology has had dazzling effects, not only by increasing longevity but also by creating the potential for improving one's quality of life. Today we are able to maintain someone who is in a persistent vegetative state with tube feedings, catheters, and ventilators. We are able to keep patients alive with dialysis treatments three days a week. We are able to "bring people back to life" with CPR and to treat infections with antibiotics and cancers with chemotherapy and radiation therapy, as well as surgery. Despite all of these advancements, humans remain mortal. There is no fountain of youth. We must be sensitive to not just the length of time someone is alive but also to the quality of life they are enduring.[15]

Americans spend an enormous amount of money on healthcare. Over the past thirty years healthcare spending has increased from 6 percent to almost 18 percent of our gross domestic product. The Centers for Medicare and Medicaid Services (CMS) estimates that Medicare expends approximately 25 percent of its budget on patient care during the last year of life.

When surveyed, most people express a desire to die at home after a short illness, but 75 percent will die in institutions.[16] Approximately 50 percent of people 65 or older will die in the hospital. Approximately 20 percent of these will die in the intensive care unit (ICU) connected to various machines such as monitors, IVs, and ventilators and heavily sedated or comatose.[17] Twenty to 25 percent die in nursing homes.[18] These numbers illustrate how far we have come from our earlier history, when patients were cared for and died at home surrounded by their families. Death has become disconnected from the living.

I have spoken with thousands of patients over my career, and I have found a recurring theme. People do not want to be kept alive if their life does not have meaning or they cannot enjoy their life. For each individual, the definition of a meaningful life varies but there are consistent themes:

- the ability to recognize and enjoy family
- the ability to eat and drink fluids
- the ability to live comfortably with minimal pain
- the ability to be self-sufficient and not be dependent on others for their care

I have never had a patient tell me they want to die while connected to multiple machines, unconscious and being kept alive by artificial nutrition and hydration. However, I have had family members tell me that is exactly what they wish for their loved one.

As Americans we need to change our ideas about the use of the technology we have today. We need to shift our focus from *cure* at all costs no matter how remote the possibility to *comfort* when it is clear the patient will never be cured or have a meaningful recovery despite maximal medical care. If studies show that most people desire to die at home but 75 percent are dying in institutions then we need to shift our focus on how we care for our loved ones in order to provide them the type of care and death they desire, a death that includes the family and those important to the patient, a death that focuses on comfort and control of symptoms, in fact a death much like it was prior to World War II.

CHAPTER 3

SURROGATE DECISION MAKERS

We cannot banish dangers, but we can banish fears. We must not demean life by standing in awe of death.
— David Sarnoff

It is highly recommended everyone have an Advance Directive and Durable Power of Attorney for Healthcare in the event they become incapacitated and are unable to make their treatment wishes known. Completing these documents is collectively called advance care planning. Advance care planning not only includes the completion of these legal documents but also involves discussions with family members and healthcare providers about how you want your beliefs and preferences to guide treatment decisions should you face a serious chronic illness or a sudden and unexpected critical illness. The focus of advance care planning is to establish what values, goals, and outcomes are important to you so that treatment or care decisions are made that support those values and goals. Advance care planning also includes designating someone, a surrogate decision maker, to make healthcare decisions for you if a time comes when you are unable to make these decisions yourself.

A surrogate decision maker (also known as an attorney in fact, healthcare proxy, or agent) is someone who makes healthcare treatment and care decisions for you if you are incapacitated or incompetent and cannot make decisions for yourself. It is best for you to designate a surrogate decision maker before you need one. Once you have made your designation, then it is important to review it periodically to make sure your surrogate decision maker is still able to act on your behalf. Like most married people, you may designate your spouse as your surrogate decision maker, but if your spouse is elderly and has his or her own health problems, these may change over time and make him or her incompetent to act on your behalf. Your spouse may even precede you in death. Therefore, you need to periodically review your advance directive and Durable Power of Attorney for Healthcare and make changes as needed.

I strongly recommend you do not leave your healthcare decisions up to chance. Designating your surrogate decision maker through an advance directive or Durable Power of Attorney for Healthcare is the best way to ensure your wishes are honored and you do not receive care or treatment that you do not want. It is important you appoint a surrogate decision maker who is comfortable with your wishes and is able to make decisions on your behalf. It will not do you any good to have someone appointed who does not respect your values and goals and will make decisions that may directly oppose your own.

Think carefully about whom you choose as your surrogate decision maker. Do not feel obligated to appoint your oldest child. Being the oldest does not automatically make him or her the best qualified. I have met many families where the surrogate decision maker was the eldest child, but for various reasons he or she had not been involved in the patient's life at all and often hadn't spoken to the patient in years. This led to poor decision making and severe conflict within the family. If a younger child is better suited to be the surrogate decision maker, then that is whom you should appoint. Birth order should not be a consideration, nor should gender. Patients often feel they should designate their oldest son as the surrogate decision maker. Many sons I have worked with through the years felt helpless and did not want to make the needed decisions. They often relied on their siblings or spouse to help them make decisions.

I have met families who were not comfortable making decisions for their loved one at all and did not want that responsibility, so they obtained a court-appointed legal guardian for the patient, even though they remained actively involved in the patient's life.

It is most important to appoint someone whom you have spoken with and who knows your wishes. You and the surrogate decision maker must be confident he or she can implement your wishes when necessary. This will lessen the emotional burden on the surrogate decision maker and ensure you receive the care you desire.

If a person is unable to speak for themselves or make decisions about their healthcare, they are considered incompetent. Incompetence may be due to immaturity, mental illness, serious brain damage, dementia, or any other condition that limits the person's ability to make informed decisions. The surrogate decision maker is designated in an advance directive or Durable Power of Attorney for Healthcare. If you do not have a legal document that designates who your surrogate decision maker is, then one is selected according to a legal hierarchy of those persons who are eligible to act as your surrogate decision maker.[1] If you have made your preferences known through an advance directive or Durable Power of Attorney for Healthcare, then the surrogate decision maker has a written document that guides him or her in making decisions for you. Without a written document, the surrogate decision maker is placed in a situation where decisions must be made with little or no knowledge of what you want for treatment and care.

If you have not designated a surrogate decision maker, then someone must step in and provide some direction for the healthcare team and make treatment decisions. The law and the Council on Ethical and Judicial Affairs for the American Medical Association[2] is clear on the hierarchy of how a surrogate decision maker is appointed. Healthcare surrogate decision makers are selected in the following order:

1. the patient's guardian
2. the patient's spouse
3. an adult child of the patient
4. either parent of the patient
5. adult sibling of the patient
6. adult grandchild of the patient
7. a close friend or other relative[3]

This is important to know. When there is a disagreement or dispute among family members as to how you should be treated or when the family cannot agree on which family member should act as the surrogate decision maker, this hierarchy is enacted. Review this order carefully. If you do not trust someone in your family to make decisions for you that are consistent with your wishes and they are high up on the list, then you may end up with the very person you don't want in charge of making decisions for you. Also, if your spouse has health issues that will keep him or her from being able to make decisions for you, then the responsibility falls to the next in line.

When a surrogate decision maker is not named in an advance directive or Durable Power of Attorney for Healthcare, then the surrogate decision maker appointed by hierarchy must use the doctrine of substituted judgment in making decisions. This means the surrogate decision maker must make decisions based on what they know the patient's wishes to be. These may have been discussed sometime in the past. They have an obligation to follow the expressed wishes of the patient and to act in the patient's best interest, taking into account any past conversations, values, and goals if known. The surrogate decision maker may make decisions that they would not make for themselves but are consistent with the patient's wishes.

If the surrogate decision maker does not have any prior knowledge of the patient's wishes then he must make best-interest decisions. Best-interest decisions are made by attempting to determine what a "rational being," a group of knowledgeable or interested persons, or society would perceive as a good outcome for the patient. The surrogate decision maker uses the family's or his or her own values in choosing treatment or care for the patient.[4] These types of decisions have been shown to be in direct conflict with what the patient wanted 30 percent of the time. Therefore it is recommended everyone complete an advance directive or Durable Power of Attorney for Healthcare in order to avoid receiving treatment they may not want. According to a study conducted in 2013 persons who appointed a Durable Power of Attorney for Healthcare were less likely to die in a hospital or receive unwanted care.[5]

Who cannot be your surrogate decision maker? The following people are denied the ability to act as a healthcare surrogate:

- the patient's treating healthcare provider

- an employee of the treating healthcare provider, unless that employee is a relative of the patient
- the owner, operator, or administrator of the patient's current healthcare facility
- an employee of an owner, operator, or administrator of the patient's current healthcare facility, unless that employee is a relative of the patient[6]

Keep this in mind when designating your surrogate decision maker. Some people do not assign a surrogate decision maker but rather rely on their physician to make the "right decision" for them. This is especially common if the patient has had a long, close relationship with their physician. Legally, your physician cannot make these decisions for you. He or she can only present you or your surrogate decision maker with the information regarding your condition and treatment options. He or she must receive treatment instructions from you or your surrogate decision maker.

You may never need to call upon a surrogate decision maker, but if you do then it is paramount you have designated someone you have confidence in to ensure you receive the treatment you desire. I recommend you do not leave this up to chance but be proactive in designating a surrogate decision maker who will act on your behalf if needed.

CHAPTER 4

ADVANCE DIRECTIVES

While I thought that I was learning how to
live, I have been learning how to die.
—Leonardo daVinci

The advance directive is an important element of advance care planning. It is a written legal document that is used by the surrogate decision maker and the healthcare team in order to ensure an incapacitated person is treated and cared for in a way that is consistent with their written wishes, values, and goals.

Advance directives were first sanctioned in 1976, and then in order to encourage the widespread use of advance directives, Congress passed the Patient Self-Determination Act in 1990, which mandated that all Medicare-certified institutions provide written information regarding a patient's right to complete an advance directive.[1] Medicare-certified institutions include hospitals, nursing homes, assisted-living facilities, long-term acute-care hospitals (LTAC), home-health and hospice agencies, and others. This act was instrumental in encouraging and allowing individuals to make a written declaration of what life-sustaining treatments they want to be continued, withheld, or withdrawn at a time when it becomes clear that further treatment will not benefit the individual or result in meaningful recovery. This is why every time you go to the hospital you are asked if you have an advance directive. The advance directive is placed in the patient's chart. With each hospitalization or admission, a check is made whether the patient has made any revisions or revoked the advance directive. This ensures the information is up to date and accurate. If you make any changes to your advance directive, you should take the revised copy with you and have it placed in your chart.

A study conducted from 2000 to 2006 showed that 42.5 percent of persons aged 65 or older needed decisions regarding healthcare be made. Of those, 70.3 percent lacked decision-making capacity. Of those lacking decision-making capacity, 67.6 percent had an advance directive. Those who had an advance directive received care that was strongly in line with their wishes. This same study reported that individuals who completed an advance directive were more likely to want limited care (92.7 percent) or comfort care (96.2 percent) than all care possible (1.9 percent). In 2010, up to 70 percent of older adults living in the community had completed an advance directive.

Advance directives are completed by an individual at a time when they have full capacity for understanding what measures they want employed, withheld or withdrawn. There are a number of considerations to bear in mind about advance directives:

- Advance directives are designed to protect patient autonomy under the belief that patients who lose decision-making capacity are more likely to receive the care they want if they document their wishes in advance, choose a surrogate decision maker, or both.
- Advance directives are invoked or enacted only when the individual has lost decision-making capacity or is considered incompetent to make decisions.

- Advance directives can only be revoked or revised by the individual who completed the advance directive (you). Your family, spouse, significant other, healthcare providers, or anyone else cannot alter, change, override, or nullify your advance directive.
- Advance directives protect you from others stepping in and authorizing treatments you have designated you do not want.
- Advance directives remove the burden of decision making on your family or another surrogate decision maker, especially if they do not have any prior knowledge of treatment options you desire.

Although it is difficult for many people to discuss end-of-life and death, advance directives, along with discussions with your family, friends, and healthcare provider, will help to make this transition smoother. Studies have shown 73 percent of surrogate decision makers experience anxiety, 35 percent experience depression, and 33 percent experience post-traumatic stress disorder (PTSD) if they have to make end-of-life decisions for their loved ones without an advance directive to guide their decision making.[2] This is one of the many important reasons why having end-of-life discussions and advance care planning is so important. Easing the burden placed on your family will ensure you receive the care you want while helping your family emotionally cope with your illness and death.

When I first started working in the hospital in the 1970s, no one had an advance directive and patients were often subjected to traumatic and futile treatments, such as cardiopulmonary resuscitation (CPR). I don't remember anyone asking the patient if he or she wanted those things done. The physician ordered tests and treatments without consulting the patient or family. Patients were told what was going to be done; they were never asked if they wanted them done. Treatments were often painful and futile and were carried out in the knowledge that they would not save the patient or even prolong life in any meaningful way. Often these treatments (such as CPR) were more of a learning tool or teachable moment for young nurses and doctors, and I believe they were done to benefit the staff and not the patient. I remember thinking as a young nurse that this was interesting, but I also had a stronger feeling that it was wrong. I felt it was disrespectful to the patient.

Advance directives are not complicated or technically difficult to complete. The most difficult part is determining the type of care you want continued, withheld, or withdrawn if you become incapacitated and cannot express your wishes or if you develop an illness that, despite the best medical care, will result in your death or severe disability.

You do not need to pay an attorney to complete an advance directive. Most institutions have a generic form with boxes for you to check. There are also forms available on the internet. The advance directive should designate which treatments you want continued, withheld, or withdrawn. The hospital or other institution will have staff available to counsel you and answer any questions you may have. The advance directive must be signed by you in front of a witness, witnessed by non-family members, and notarized to order to make it valid. Of course, if you choose you can consult an attorney to help you with completing your advance directive.

Over the years I have realized that most people are very strong in their convictions about what they do or do not want in regard to life-sustaining treatments. Many patients express that they never want to be placed on machines, have a feeding tube, or "have a tube down my throat."

Whenever you need to make changes, it is preferable to complete a new advance directive rather than making changes on the existing form. One day while I was working in the emergency department of a local hospital, a patient arrived in cardiac arrest, and his wife brought a copy of his advance directive. Unfortunately, his advance directive had so many changes with items scratched out and penciled in and notes written in the margins that no one was certain what the patient wanted, and this made the advance directive useless. Thankfully, his wife was able to provide guidance and make decisions regarding his treatment and thus ensured he received the type of care he wanted.

Typical Types of Treatment Addressed in an Advance Directive

What types of treatment can be addressed in an advance directive? They include the following:

- CPR (chest compressions and defibrillation)
- mechanical ventilation, which includes intubation and placement on a ventilator (respirator)
- antibiotics
- artificial nutrition and hydration
- placement of feeding tubes
- surgery
- chemotherapy
- radiation therapy
- blood transfusions

If you are using a generic form, there will be a blank space or spaces to add anything else not specifically listed that you may or may not want. Some patients opt to place a statement in their advance directive about the option of trying specific treatments with withdrawal or discontinuation of the treatment after a few days if they do not improve or benefit from the treatment. This is a reasonable approach and is employed often. I have found this helps the family in coming to terms with the patient's illness and helps them to know they "did all they could" for the patient while still honoring their loved one's wishes.

Considerations When Determining Treatment Options

When considering what treatments you may want continued, withheld, or withdrawn, there are several considerations to keep in mind.

How effective is the treatment and what are its goals? Will treatment potentially cure your illness? If not, will treatment contribute to your comfort or improve your quality of life? Will treatment allow you more time with your loved ones without causing more suffering or pain?

How old is the patient? It is important to consider where we are in our life span. The older we are, the less likely it is that interventions will be effective or lead to an increase in life expectancy. Risk factors for poor survival after CPR include being seventy years old or more. Studies have shown that rates of survival after CPR to being able to be discharged to home are low and have not changed substantially since 1992. The rates of out-of-hospital CPR with survival to discharge ranged between 8.5 and 9.6 percent in one study, and 6.7 and 8.4 in another study. Survival rates to discharge after CPR while in the hospital was not much better at approximately 17 percent.[3] Prior residence in a skilled nursing facility worsens the chance of survival after CPR.

Other considerations apply if you are of an advanced age. Individuals aged 85 and older have only a 6 percent chance of survival after CPR. Advanced age also reduces your treatment options and poses greater risk of side effects and poor outcomes without significantly improving life expectancy.

Other comorbidities reduce the effectiveness of all treatments and chances of survival, including renal failure with or without dialysis, congestive heart failure, hepatic (liver) insufficiency, acute stroke, immunodeficiency, severe disability, coma, or vegetative state.

Cancer worsens the likelihood of survival after CPR. Cancer patients have an overall survival rate of 6.2 percent, and rates are even lower if they have metastatic disease, hematologic malignancies, or a history of stem-cell transplant. Cancer patients whose hospital course followed a path of gradual deterioration have a zero percent survival rate after CPR.[4]

What about quality of life? If the severity of the disease will prohibit the patient from participating in life in any meaningful way, then treatment is often withheld or withdrawn. Artificial nutrition and hydration is frequently declined. Many people do not want to be maintained on artificial nutrition and hydration merely to be "alive" without any recognition of their surroundings or family. They do not want to have a feeding tube placed and then potentially have their family have to decide whether to discontinue the tube feedings at a later date. The ability to enjoy food and fluid orally is paramount to some. They do not want to live if they cannot eat or enjoy a cup of coffee or a glass of wine. I once treated a delightful 94-year-old grandmother. Mrs. R.K. suffered a stroke that left her unable to swallow. Therefore, she could not eat any food or drink any fluids, which meant she would require a feeding tube to provide artificial nutrition and hydration. After discussing her treatment options, she decided she did not want a feeding tube placed. She decided she wanted palliative care and to be kept comfortable, and she refused any further treatment. Mrs. R.K. had a very attentive grandson who became distraught at her decision. He explained to me that he had promised her she would live to be 100. Unfortunately, her grandson had made a promise that neither he nor anyone else could keep. Mrs. R.K. gently informed her grandson that she did not want to live to be 100. She was content with the life she had had up to the time of the stroke, and she was looking forward to seeing her husband, who had died many years earlier.

It is not enough to complete an advance directive. You need to make sure your advance directive is accessible to those who need it. An advance directive is a legal document that works only if people know it exists and can read it. It does not belong in your safe deposit box. Patients have told me they keep their advance directive in their safe deposit box so they know where it is. This is the absolute worst place for your advance directive! It makes your advance directive useless, because no one can read it and know what type of care you want. If something happens to you, you cannot go to the bank and get your advance directive, and there may not be anyone else who has access to your safe deposit box. Even if your spouse is able to go to the bank, access to the box is limited. It can only be accessed during bank business hours. You may be out of town when you become ill and be miles away from your bank. Having your advance directive in your safe deposit box is tantamount to not having one at all.

Do not keep your advance directive in your attorney's office. I have met many patients who do not have a copy of their own, but have their attorney keep a copy in his office. Again, this is a very bad idea. As luck would have it, the patient invariably is admitted to the hospital after routine business hours or on a weekend or holiday, which makes the advance directive unavailable until the following business day. I have even had an attorney who could not find the advance directive once they were contacted! So once again, the advance directive was useless. Please give a copy of your advance directive to your physician or healthcare provider, the hospital, your spouse, and your surrogate decision maker. This ensures someone will have a copy when it is needed.

I live in the Midwest where it is very cold in the winter. Many people go south for the winter. An advance directive is portable, meaning you can take it with you wherever you go. Women should keep a copy in their purse. You should take a copy with you when you go on vacation, and if you are a snowbird, take a copy with you wherever you spend your winter months. If you are out of state and become ill, you will be treated by a healthcare team that is not familiar with you, and they may institute treatment not knowing that you have designated that you do not want it. Remember, an advance directive only works as long as it is available and can be reviewed by those taking care of you.

Advance directives are an effective legal method of ensuring you receive the type of healthcare you desire when you are unable to discuss your healthcare options and treatments. If you do not want to complete an advance directive or make these decisions yourself, a Durable Power of Attorney for Healthcare is a good option or alternative in ensuring you receive the type of care you desire. This will be discussed in the next chapter.

If you are having difficulty talking to your loved ones about your end-of-life choices, there is a website, theconversationproject. org, that can help you start the conversation with your family.

State-specific advance directives can be obtained by accessing the National Hospice and Palliative Care Organization Caring Connections website at www.NHPCO.org.

CHAPTER 5

DURABLE POWER OF ATTORNEY FOR HEALTHCARE AND FINANCES

No evil is honorable; but death is honorable;
therefore death is not evil.
—Citium Zeno

A Durable Power of Attorney is a written legal document that authorizes someone to represent you or act on your behalf when you become incapacitated. Unlike an ordinary or "nondurable" power of attorney, the Durable Power of Attorney remains in effect once you become incapacitated and therefore your designated agent or surrogate decision maker can act on your behalf. We will discuss two types of Durable Power of Attorney, the Durable Power of Attorney for Healthcare and the Durable Power of Attorney for Finances.

A Durable Power of Attorney for Healthcare will allow your surrogate decision maker or agent to legally make treatment decisions for you. A Durable Power of Attorney for Finances will allow your agent to legally manage your finances, including paying your bills, managing your investments, and buying or selling assets. I recommend that everyone have a Durable Power of Attorney for Healthcare as well as a Durable Power of Attorney for Finances. You do not need to name the same person as your agent or surrogate decision maker for both. In fact, you may want to keep the two separate to avoid any conflict of interest. Everyone has his or her own particular strengths. You may trust your eldest child to make sound healthcare decisions for you, but he may not be good at managing finances. In that situation you should appoint someone else to look after your finances. A non-family member such as an attorney or accountant is often chosen as the agent for a Durable Power of Attorney for Finances. Although both types can be included in the same document, I recommend that you have two separate documents rather than combining them together. The Durable Power of Attorney for Finances may include sensitive information about your finances and personal information that you do not want shared. Therefore it is best to keep this separate. Your hospital, healthcare providers, and caregivers do not need this information.

I will focus on the Durable Power of Attorney for Healthcare. Why should you have a Durable Power of Attorney for Healthcare? For many of the same reasons you should have an advance directive. The Durable Power of Attorney for Healthcare designates someone as your surrogate decision maker or agent to act on your behalf and make healthcare decisions for you if you are incapacitated. You can also designate an alternate agent if the first is not available. The Durable Power of Attorney for Healthcare differs from an advance directive in that you do not have to be as specific about your treatment wishes as you do in an advance directive. It is a good alternative for someone who is uncomfortable in making healthcare treatment decisions without knowing what the future may hold for them. Some people specifically designate in their Durable Power of Attorney for Healthcare which treatments they want continued, withdrawn, or withheld just like in their advance directive. Others leave the treatment decisions solely up to their designated agent. I have found that these patients typically do not want to discuss the possibility of death and do not want to make decisions as they "cannot predict the future." They would rather have someone else make decisions for them at the appropriate time—someone who will have all the information they need to make informed treatment or care decisions. Just like the advance directive, a copy of your Durable Power of Attorney for Healthcare should be given to all those who are involved in your care.

It is important that the person you designate as your surrogate decision maker or agent is comfortable with the responsibility you are bestowing upon him or her, particularly if you do not want to designate your preferences, as this will give your agent the sole responsibility for making healthcare decisions on your behalf without any guidance from you. If you have spoken with your agent about any preferences you may have, this will help guide decision making in the future.

A study which followed the families of terminally ill patients found that these families often found decision making difficult. Some families could not make a decision to limit treatment because of the emotional pain it would cause them to know that they had decided to let a loved one die from his or her terminal illness. Having a Durable Power of Attorney for Healthcare will help to reduce the stress of decision making on your family and agent if you specify your preferences. Honoring a loved one's wishes decreases the stress associated with end-of-life decision making and can reduce the negative impact of making difficult end-of-life decisions on behalf of a loved one. The following are recommended qualities to look for when choosing a Durable Power of Attorney for Healthcare:

- He or she meets the legal criteria for appointing a proxy/healthcare agent.
- He or she is willing to speak on behalf of the patient.
- He or she is able to act on the patient's wishes and separate his or her own feelings.
- He or she lives close by or could travel if needed.
- He or she knows the patient well and understands what is important to the patient.
- He or she could handle the responsibility, physically and emotionally.
- He or she will talk with the patient now about sensitive issues.
- He or she will be available in the future if needed.
- He or she is able to handle conflicting opinions among family members, friends, or medical personnel.[1]

Just as when you are setting up your advance directive, you should carefully consider whom you designate as your agent or surrogate decision maker in your Durable Power of Attorney for Healthcare. Do not let birth order or other extraneous factors influence your decision. Choose the person you know will have your best interests at heart.

You may designate an alternate agent in the event your first agent is unavailable or unable to make decisions for you. This is particularly important if your assigned surrogate decision maker or agent is your spouse. If you are elderly, it is likely your spouse is elderly as well and may have health issues such as dementia that have evolved since you completed your Durable Power of Attorney for Healthcare, and this may make him or her unsuitable to make decisions on your behalf. It is important to include the contact information for your surrogate decision maker or agent so that healthcare personnel know how to get in touch with him or her if needed. Periodically review this information and update it as needed. It does not do you any good to appoint someone who cannot be found or reached when needed.

Do not co-appoint or designate more than one agent simultaneously. I have encountered patients who have designated equally all their children in a Durable Power of Attorney for Healthcare. The intention was not show to favoritism or to keep a child from feeling left out. This is a disaster! It is an impossible situation that almost guarantees that your wishes will not be honored. It is just like when a group of people cannot agree on which restaurant to go to for dinner. The same thing can happen with treatment decisions, only on a larger and more tragic scale where the stakes are much higher. You, the patient, are the pawn in this situation, and oftentimes you may receive treatment you do not want. I have seen this happen. It leads to a hostile environment with conflict, arguments, and hard feelings among those holding joint Durable Power of Attorney which may cause a permanent rift among them.

If your children have never been able to get along or agree on anything, then please do not expect them to get along and agree on your treatment and care. This is an emotional and stressful time for families, and decision making can be difficult. Don't worry about upsetting or offending anyone. This is about you and what you want. This is about you receiving or not receiving treatment for an acute or chronic illness. If just one of the multiply assigned Durable Power of Attorneys disagrees with the treatment plan, the healthcare team is obligated to continue aggressive treatment you may not want.

I have met many families of patients over the years who were relieved there was a Durable Power of Attorney for Healthcare designated, as this kept them from having to make difficult decisions. They were happy to defer all decisions to the Durable Power of Attorney, and they could focus on providing emotional and psychological support for their loved one.

Assign only one Durable Power of Attorney for Healthcare. Designate an alternate in the event the first agent is unavailable or unable to make the necessary decisions. Make sure each person designated is clear on what your end-of-life preferences are if you know them, and make sure your agent is capable and comfortable when it comes to implementing your preferences. If your agent expresses doubt about being able to implement your wishes, then you need to assign someone else as your agent.

A Durable Power of Attorney for Healthcare, just like an advance directive, can not only reduce family stress when making decisions for a loved one but will also ensure that your wishes are being followed and you receive care consistent with your values and goals.

CHAPTER 6

DETERMINING THE LEVEL OF CARE

*It is impossible that anything so natural, so necessary,
and so universal as death, should ever have been
designed by providence as an evil to mankind.*
—Jonathan Swift

When we are initially faced with an illness whether it is acute and of a short duration or a chronic illness such as diabetes, kidney failure, or hypertension, we immediately think about needing treatment. We think of what the doctor can do to make us better. What medications, surgery, or treatment can help us feel better and improve our life? What will help us get back to work and our family? What will provide the fastest treatment and recovery? What will make us live longer? How much will it cost?

How do you know what type of treatment you would want? I believe the answer is highly dependent on where you are in your life and in achieving your life goals and whether a life-threatening disease is sudden (acute), such as a new diagnosis of cancer, or chronic, such as congestive heart failure, chronic obstructive pulmonary disease, or diabetes. My career has been spent mostly with adults who are in their wage-earning or retirement years of life. My experience has been that the younger the patient, the more likely they will want all types of care possible, with little discussion of the possibility of death. Death is not an option, at least initially. This is especially true if the disease is cancer which everyone is afraid of. A diagnosis of cancer brings out all our fears. Fear of not being around for our children who may still be young. Fear of missing out on important life events such as graduations, weddings, births of children, grandchildren and loss of control over one's life. Fear of the unknown. Fear of death. What awaits us when we die?

At first, there is the goal to win—to defeat the disease, to be triumphant over death. Discussions are often focused around treatment and surveillance of the effectiveness of treatment to demonstrate victory over the disease. When disease progresses despite maximal appropriate treatment, the goal will often change from focusing on cure to realizing that the patient may not survive and focusing on how his or her family and loved ones will continue in the event of death.

Those who have lived longer, especially those over seventy-five, may feel they have experienced life, lived a good life, and accomplished their life goals. Older adults may have lost a spouse, may find living alone difficult or unbearable, and may look forward to seeing their beloved husband or wife again. They may be more willing to discuss the possibility that they may not survive. They are also more willing to discuss the risk versus the benefit of treatments for someone of their age, especially if they have coexisting chronic diseases that make treatment more difficult and increase the risk of adverse complications. Depending on their age and other chronic diseases they may have, aggressive treatment may not be an option. They are more likely to opt for minimal treatment to control symptoms and keep them comfortable.

Family also plays a role in determining what treatments a patient will undergo. Family members of a younger person will often be their cheerleaders, encouraging them to fight and beat the disease. They cannot accept the possibility of losing their loved one at a young age, when they still have "so much life ahead of them." Families of older adults may also initially want the patient to submit to all treatment possible, but they are more willing to consider the possibility that the patient may not make it. They realize that advanced age makes treatment more difficult or even impossible. They also seem to be more willing to accept decisions the patient makes regarding treatment, even if it means limiting treatment. The older adult is less likely to be pressured into submitting to treatment he or she may not want.

This is not to say a life-threatening disease such as cancer is easier on families of older adults. They still have all the same fears that families of younger adults have, including the fear of losing a loved one and of how they will continue on without them. They may be concerned their loved one will suffer or be in pain.

There isn't any right or wrong answer when determining how much care or treatment an individual receives. Each answer and treatment plan is as unique as the person faced with making the decision. It is important to discuss all your options with a physician or healthcare provider you feel comfortable with, someone who is able to discuss the pros and cons of available treatment, how your new diagnosis impacts your health, and how other comorbid diseases you have affect your treatment options.

Communication with your healthcare team is key to having the best experience possible in planning and implementing your treatment and its follow-up throughout the rest of your life. Treatment does not just address the immediate effects and expectations; it also involves the long-range effects of treatment and what you can expect. All of this information will help you to make an informed decision regarding your treatment options.

There are many factors to be taken into consideration other than age whenever we are faced with a disease, whether it is an acute or chronic:

- preexisting chronic or comorbid conditions
- the ability to care for oneself or ability to do activities of daily living without assistance
- the level of dependency on others for care
- the prognosis

As mentioned earlier, age is important in considering whether to pursue treatment, especially with a new diagnosis of a life-threatening disease such as cancer. The majority of cancer diagnoses and deaths occur in people older than 65. It is anticipated that 70 percent of all cancers will occur in those 65 and older by the year 2030.

Comorbid conditions have implications for treatment options and success. The severity of comorbidities affects overall survival. In a study of 7,600 cancer patients older than 55, those between the ages of 55 and 64 had an average of 2.9 chronic (comorbid) diseases, whereas patients aged 75 and older had an average of 4.2 comorbid diseases. Comorbid diseases may increase the risks associated with treatment, decrease the effectiveness of treatment, or eliminate certain types of treatment altogether.[1]

The inability to care for oneself and participate in activities of daily living is often cited by the patients I have known as a reason for limiting treatment. When patients are unable to participate in functions or activities that give them pleasure, they often do not want to submit to treatments that may not improve their quality of life and may worsen what quality they have due to side effects of treatment. They often state they do not want to be a burden on their family.

Prognosis is to be considered when making treatment decisions. Will the treatment improve your chance of survival, and if not, will it improve your quality of life by controlling symptoms? Just because a treatment is available, it doesn't mean you have to do it. If treatment is recommended but will not have any benefit or contribute to your life expectancy or comfort, then you may want to consider withholding that treatment.

Once a treatment has been initiated, it does not mean that you cannot change your mind and stop the treatment. However, this is easier said than done. I believe decisions to withdraw treatment are the most difficult decisions people make. Patients often feel committed to continuing a treatment once they have consented to it, no matter how futile it is or how bad it makes them feel. The patient and family often feel like they are "giving up" if they withdraw treatment. They often don't want to disappoint their doctor or loved ones or to make them angry by stopping treatment. Family members may feel angry and worry that you don't love them if you do not consent to all treatment possible. Letting them know that you love them and how important they are to you will help them in this stressful time. Let them know you are not abandoning them but are taking the path that you know is the right path for you. Your decisions are your own to make. You are the one who knows yourself best and what you want and need. This is your life and you are the navigator. You control the direction your treatment and life take.

Treatment decisions are difficult and fraught with fear and uncertainty. We must take comfort in knowing that the decisions we make are the right decisions at the time they are made. We shouldn't second guess ourselves. This doesn't mean we can't change our minds later. Throughout life we make decisions daily, and as life evolves we often change our minds and our path. The same is true when we are ill. We choose a path, but that path is winding and flexible. We may change our path at any time, whether that path includes all care possible, withholding or withdrawing care, or caring only for control of symptoms through palliative care or hospice care.

Palliative Care

With the advances in medicine, critics such as Dr. Elisabeth Kübler-Ross feared the medicalization of dying. She was concerned that the changing role of the family from that of caregiver to that of spectator, as well as the advent of mechanical ventilators, dialysis, CPR, new surgical options, medications, and other interventions, would lead to a loss of the ability to accept death and dying as normal. She was concerned that technology would lead to a rejection of the importance of personal and family care at the end of life, a disregard for traditional religious and cultural rituals surrounding death and dying, and medical control of the dying person as a patient rather than as a person. Because of these concerns, she promoted fostering the dignity of the dying person. This was the foundation for the palliative care movement.[2]

The terms "palliative care" and "hospice care" are often used interchangeably in the United States, as they have been at the hospitals where I have worked, but there is a difference between them.

The term palliative care originates from the Latin word *palliare*, which means "to cloak." Dr. Balfour Mound of Canada is credited with the first use of the term "palliative care" in 1974. It is defined as treatment given with the goal of symptom relief. Palliative care is a multidisciplinary specialty that is delivered to all patients with a complex, chronic, or life-threatening illness.[3] Palliative care may be given concurrently with treatments delivered while the patient is seeking a cure.

The World Health Organization describes palliative care as "an approach that improves the quality of life of patients and their families facing the problems associated with life-threatening illness, through the prevention and relief of suffering by means of early identification and impeccable assessment and treatment of pain and other problems, physical, psychosocial and spiritual. Palliative care affirms life and regards dying as a normal process ... intends neither to hasten nor postpone death."[4] The distinction between palliative care and hospice care is that a patient may receive palliative care while still being actively treated or while seeking a cure for his or her disease. Palliative care is aimed at symptom control, whether the symptoms are a result of the disease or a result of the treatment the patient is receiving.

Hospice Care

Hospice care is a subset of palliative care that recognizes that the patient is no longer seeking treatment or a cure from a life-threatening illness or chronic disease but is seeking relief from the symptoms with the goal of experiencing a good death that is free from suffering, while surrounded by those who love and care for him or her. As we have seen previously, most patients when asked prefer to die at home rather than in an institution, and hospice care can be provided in the home.

It is my experience here in the United States, the terms palliative care and hospice care are used interchangeably, and there is no distinction made between the two. Therefore, when discussing end-of-life decisions, the physicians, nurses, clergy, and others involved in you or your loved one's care may use these two terms to mean the same thing. In European countries, a distinction remains between the two.

In hospitals in the United States a trend has emerged to use the term "supportive care" rather than "palliative care." Therefore you may encounter this term at the hospital where you or a loved one is receiving care.

CHAPTER 7

HOSPICE CARE

Those who have the strength and the love to sit with a
dying patient in the silence that goes beyond words will
know that this moment is neither frightening nor painful,
but a peaceful cessation of the functioning of the body.
—Elisabeth Kübler-Ross

The Role of Hospice Care

The goal of today's hospice is to alleviate symptoms, to reduce unneeded and unwanted medical interventions, to improve the quality of life for the terminally ill, to attend to the physical, psychological, social, and spiritual needs of the patient and family, and ultimately to provide the patient with a good death.[1]

Patients and families have often expressed to me their fears regarding the end-of-life experience. The two most common fears I have heard are the fear of pain or suffering and the fear of feeling short of breath or of suffocating. Other fears expressed include the fears of feeling alone, losing control, and leaving loved ones behind. Patients may express concerns about their family being angry with them for "giving up." I cared for a delightful woman, Ms. H.J., a retired nurse who had battled multiple chronic diseases over several years

43

and had exceeded all her physician's expectations for survival. She had endured multiple hospitalizations and surgeries over the years. During her last hospitalization she was not responding to treatment, and therefore she decided she wanted all treatments discontinued and requested her care be changed to comfort measures only. She also requested that these measures be implemented before her daughter was notified. She knew her daughter would not agree with her decision and would be angry with her. She knew her daughter would accuse her of giving up, and she did not want to have to endure her daughter's anger. Ms. H.J. was placed on hospice care in the hospital, and then, according to her wishes, her daughter was notified. Just as Ms. H.J. anticipated, her daughter was angry that she did not have an opportunity to speak with her mother before she was placed on hospice care. After the daughter had received help to cope with her mother's decision, she was able to be supportive and spend time with her mother before she died a few days later.

An advantage of the hospice approach is that not only are those who work in hospice specialists in comfort and treating distressing symptoms, but they are also specialists in helping the patient and family work through all these concerns. Hospice gives the patient and family the opportunity to prepare for death. It allows people to resolve interpersonal conflicts that have been left incomplete. It also allows for review of their lives, perhaps to find meaning.[2] By treating the patient and the family as a unit, hospice represents a shift in the philosophy of care delivery from a "cure" model to a "comfort" model.[3] Death is acknowledged and is not seen as the enemy but as an acceptable outcome, and the goal is for the patient to experience a good death.

A good death has been described as a death with minimal pain, one that matches patient and family preferences, one with friends and family, one not being a burden, one being listened to, being able to decide about medical treatments, being treated with respect, and having the opportunity to "put one's affairs in order." A good death is less distressing for the patient and encompasses social, psychological, and philosophical aspects, such as maintaining close contacts with family during the final days and accepting one's impending death. It also allows the patient to achieve spiritual fulfillment. Studies have shown that 90 percent of hospice patients were most concerned with finding strength in their beliefs and finding comfort in faith. Patients wanted to know that their families appreciated them and that they would be able to express their feelings and say goodbye to family and friends.[4]

Recognizing the natural process of death and having open discussions about the patient's terminal illness allows the patient and family to fulfill these needs prior to death. The patient and family are educated about the process of dying and death.[5] The patient is the central figure in making decisions regarding the care he or she wishes to receive in the end stages of life. Studies have found that patients who were informed about their health conditions showed better adaptation to the disease. Full information helped patients accept their disease and utilize the resources they needed to deal with their illness. Full disclosure also allowed patients the opportunity to clarify their doubts and fears, thus reducing uncertainty and allowing practical and emotional adaptations to the illness.[6] A 2005 study found that within twenty days of admission to hospice, patients rated their quality of life as good to very good. There was a positive correlation with symptom relief, such as pain and shortness of breath and quality of life. There was also a positive correlation of spiritual and psychological well-being for those receiving hospice care.[7]

An interdisciplinary team delivers hospice care along with family and friends. The team may have the following members:

- physicians
- nurses

- social workers
- clergy
- respiratory therapists
- physical therapists
- occupational therapists
- speech therapists
- volunteers
- bereavement counselors
- respite caregivers

(To receive Medicare reimbursement, hospices are mandated to maintain a volunteer staff equal to at least five percent of the patient-care hours of all paid employees.[8])

Hospice care does not hasten death nor prolong dying.[9] In some instances hospice has been shown to lengthen life.[10] Hospice is not euthanasia, nor is it assisted suicide. Hospice is a philosophy of providing comfort and assistance to the patient and family during the natural process of dying. The goal is the comfort of the patient and the relief of symptoms and suffering associated with their terminal illness. Euthanasia and assisted suicide have a different goal in that they are aimed at bringing death about intentionally.[11]

History of Hospice Care

The word "hospice" originates from the Latin word *hospes*, which referred to either a traveling guest or a traveler's host.[12] The Crusaders in the eleventh century are credited with opening the first hospices for the incurably ill. At that time people with incurable diseases were not admitted to establishments of healing. They were viewed as a detriment to the recovery of others. The first hospices were places where travelers to and from the Holy Land were cared for and refreshed. Travelers, as well as the sick and dying, were cared for. The Knights Hospitallers of St. John of Jerusalem founded a way station in Jerusalem in the fourteenth century for sick and weary pilgrims and the terminally ill. This is the first known hospice-type facility.[13]

The first hospices were reliant on religious orders to provide care, and this tradition continued into the nineteenth century. However, over time there was less emphasis on the care of travelers and more toward the care of patients with one or two common diagnoses such as tuberculosis or cancer.[14]

Dame Cicely Saunders of the United Kingdom, a nurse, social worker, and later a physician, is credited with launching the modern hospice movement. Early in her career she decided she wanted to dedicate her life to the care of the dying. She founded St. Christopher's Hospice in London in 1967. Her goal for the hospice was to bring dignity and comfort to the dying through an interdisciplinary approach to end-of-life care. Dr. Saunders was instrumental in forming the tenets used in hospices around the world today. These include the concept of "total pain" (including physical, spiritual, and psychological discomfort), the proper use of opioids (narcotic pain medication) for patients with physical pain, and attention to the needs of family members and friends who provide care for the dying.[15]

In 1969 Dr. Elisabeth Kübler-Ross published her book *On Death and Dying*, which was instrumental in starting a conversation about the care of patients who were dying. Dr. Kübler-Ross interviewed hundreds of terminally ill patients. One of the themes that emerged was the feeling of isolation in the dying experience. Patients expressed the desire to be able to talk to someone about their diagnosis, their feelings, and their fears, but with the attitude of the day, the possibility of death was not easily acknowledged nor discussed. Information was often withheld from patients regarding their diagnosis and prognosis. Despite this, patients knew when they were dying; they did not need to be told. However, this lack of communication led to feelings of isolation, as they weren't able to discuss or share their experiences with anyone, including their family, physician, nurses, or other caregivers.

Dying patients were a reminder of our own mortality, and, as I mentioned earlier, the death of a patient was viewed as a failure of modern medicine. Death and dying were taboo topics and were not discussed. Dr. Kübler-Ross's work was instrumental in bringing to light the suffering and isolation of those dying and to bring recognition that dying is a natural process that everyone must eventually go through.

In 1967 Dr. Saunders gave a lecture to medical students, nurses, social workers, and chaplains at Yale University on the concept of holistic hospice care. As a result of this lecture Dr. Florence Wald, head of the school of nursing, along with Dr. Kübler-Ross, worked to advance hospice care in the United States. These two women were instrumental in changing the way we perceive care of the terminally ill. They promoted taking control of decision making about treatment away from the physician or institution and giving it to the patient and family. Dr. Kübler-Ross testified before a U.S. Senate Special Committee on Aging in 1972, where she proposed treatment at the end of life should remain the patient's preference. Patients should be offered alternatives to institutionalization. She stated, "We isolate both the dying and the old, and it serves a purpose. They are reminders of our own mortality. We should not institutionalize people. We can give families more help with home care and visiting nurses, giving the families and the patients the spiritual, emotional, and financial help to facilitate the final care at home."

In 1974 Dr. Wald opened the first hospice in the United States in New Haven, Connecticut. This first hospice was funded by the National Cancer Institute. The New Haven hospice was deemed a success and was recognized as providing a vital service. Soon more hospices were opened. The first hospices in the 1970s and early 1980s were staffed by volunteers and were largely intended to care for terminally ill cancer patients.[16]

In 1982 Congress passed the Medicare Hospice Benefit clause, which made hospice a benefit covered by Medicare. With this new benefit, the number of hospices grew explosively. In 1984 there were thirty-one Medicare-certified hospices in operation. In 2012 there were 5,560 Medicare- and non-Medicare-certified hospices in operation. This represents a total of 1.5 to 1.6 million users of hospice in 2012, costing Medicare $13.8 billion.

Hospice is also a covered benefit under Medicaid in forty-nine of the fifty states. The exception is Oklahoma, which provides hospice benefits to children only, not adults. All states must offer hospice benefits to children under the Medicaid Early Periodic Screening, Diagnosis, and Treatment Program (EPSDT) benefit requirement. Medicaid expenditures for hospice in 2012 were $2.44 billion.

Initially hospice focused only on the care of cancer patients who were terminally ill. This has changed over the years in recognition that people are dying of chronic diseases. In 1992 76 percent of all hospice patients had a cancer diagnosis. By 2012 this number had dropped to 36.9 percent, with non-cancer diagnoses accounting for 63.1 percent of hospice enrollee diagnoses.[17] In 2009 the top ten diagnoses for admission to hospice included only two cancer diagnoses, those being lung and colorectal cancer. The remaining eight top-ranking diagnoses for admission to hospice included the following conditions:

- debility non specified
- non-Alzheimer's dementia
- congestive heart failure
- non-infectious respiratory diseases such as COPD
- failure to thrive

- heart disease other than congestive heart failure
- Alzheimer's dementia
- stroke[18]

Eligibility Criteria for Enrollment in Hospice under Medicare

How is one eligible for hospice? The adult patient population is the one I have the most experience with in discussing and enrolling patients in hospice. These are primarily patients enrolled in Medicare or Medicaid, and therefore this information will focus on Medicare rules for hospice. There has been a marketing push by private insurance companies such as Blue Cross/Blue Shield, Anthem, Cigna, and others to enroll those 65 years and older into "Medicare replacement or Medicare Advantage policies." These policies are promoted as less expensive and are therefore intended to appeal to those 65 and older on a limited budget. However, the old adage "you get what you pay for" applies here, and I encourage you to review the coverage of these policies thoroughly before changing from Medicare to a private Medicare replacement policy. These policies do not have the same coverage as Medicare. They vary in the coverage they will provide and the deductibles and co-payments for which you may be responsible. There are too many variations to cover here, and this coverage may change yearly.

To be eligible for hospice under Medicare, you must meet the following criteria.[19]

- You must be entitled to Part A of Medicare.
- You must have decided that you no longer want treatment to cure your terminal illness or your doctor must have determined that efforts to cure your illness are futile.

- You must sign a statement choosing hospice care instead of routine Medicare-covered benefits for your terminal illness. This statement indicates that you will not return to the hospital for curative treatment of your terminal illness.
- Your hospice physician must certify that you have a terminal illness with a life-expectancy of six months or less if the disease follows its natural course.

If you or your family member lives longer than six months, hospice care can continue if your physician re-certifies your terminal diagnosis. I did meet one patient who had been enrolled in hospice for two years, and although this was very unusual, she was able to continue in hospice with the required re-certifications by her hospice physician.

Once enrolled in hospice care, all treatments or tests that are not specifically for symptom control will be discontinued, including X-rays, CT scans, EKGs, laboratory tests (blood draws), and medications intended to treat or cure your terminal illness. Any treatments that are for symptom control or comfort will be continued. Once enrolled in hospice, you do have the right to stop or opt out of hospice care at any time.

Types of Hospice Care

We've discussed hospice as a concept and an interdisciplinary team, but where is hospice? Where do you go to get hospice? Hospice can occur in multiple settings. In the United Kingdom, hospice is primarily provided in hospice facilities which provide a homey atmosphere and skilled staff to care for the patient. There are some inpatient hospice facilities in the United States, but these are few. Not every city has an inpatient hospice facility where you can be cared for. Where I live we do not have a hospice facility in the community, and therefore the majority of hospice occurs in the home.

There are four types or categories of Medicare hospice care:

- routine home care
- continuous home care
- inpatient respite care
- general inpatient care

Routine Home Hospice Care

The majority of hospice services are provided in the home as routine home care. In 2010 97.3 percent of all hospice days were in the home.[20] In the home the patient is cared for by family or friends. The interdisciplinary hospice team comes into the home for periods of time to assist and provide medical expertise and guidance, as well as emotional and spiritual support for the patient and the family. The hospice team is available twenty-four hours a day, seven days a week by telephone and is available for emergency visits in addition to routine scheduled visits.

Someone must be designated as the primary caregiver, and someone must be with the patient twenty-four hours a day while the patient is enrolled in hospice in the home. This responsibility can be shared by multiple family members with one person "organizing" all the others. Families often devise shifts when they will be in the home with the patient in order to have continuous care.

Having hospice in the home requires a team approach. The hospice team, in conjunction with the patient and family, devises a plan of care that includes not only the patient but also the family, as they are considered a unit. The hospice team then evaluates the patient's and family's response to the plan of care, including evaluation of symptom control, the comfort of the patient, and the patient's and family's coping and support. The hospice team does not stay twenty-four hours a day but is available if needed.

In-home hospice is not recommended if there is only one caregiver, as this would be too physically and emotionally exhausting for the caregiver. I have met many an elderly spouse who has taken on full responsibility for the care of their terminally ill spouse. Although this is admirable, it often leads to caregivers becoming exhausted and having to be admitted to the hospital for treatment of their own chronic diseases that they tend to neglect in an effort to care for the patient. I have also met elderly patients who have died while caring for their ill spouse. They are distraught, not about their own impending death but about who will care for their ill spouse once they die.

Continuous Home Hospice Care

Continuous home hospice care is provided by hospice staff, but this is limited to periods of patient crisis. Continuous hospice care can be provided in long-term care facilities such as nursing homes and assisted living facilities. In this situation the staff of the facility and the hospice staff work collaboratively to provide care for the patient. Hospice staff members work with the staff of the facility to develop and implement a plan of care for the patient and family. Some patients and families opt for hospice in a long-term care facility. If the patient was already residing in a long-term care facility at the time of their terminal diagnosis, this is a natural extension of care in their "home," as the facility is considered the patient's home. Also, patients who do not have family who are able to care for them may be admitted to a long-term care facility in order to receive hospice services.

The advantages to hospice in a long-term care facility include fewer unnecessary hospitalizations, improved pain management, fewer invasive procedures such as physical restraints and IV infusions, and greater family satisfaction with care, as well as twenty-four hour access to skilled staff.[21] It also reduces the burden of caregiving on the family.

As I mentioned previously, the family may not be physically or emotionally able to care for the patient for various reasons, which may include poor physical health or a lack of family availability to be with the patient twenty-four hours a day. Some people are not comfortable caring for a terminally ill family member. I have had children tell me they don't want to care for their mother or father as it would be too upsetting. They want to remember them as they were before they became ill. The number of hospice patients residing in nursing facilities has increased from 11 percent in 1992 to 36 percent in 2000.

General Inpatient Hospice Care

General inpatient care is when the patient is admitted to the hospital on the recommendation of the hospice team for treating symptoms that cannot be managed in another setting such as the home or long-term care facility. This is a short hospitalization for symptom management only, and once symptoms have been controlled and a plan for continuing symptom management has been developed, the patient is discharged to home or a long-term care facility. The patient can be admitted to the hospital only at the recommendation of the hospice team; otherwise the hospitalization will not be covered by Medicare.

Inpatient Respite Hospice Care

Inpatient respite hospice care is provided in a hospital or facility in order to provide respite (a break or rest period) for the caregiver or family. Inpatient respite care can be provided in a hospital, a skilled nursing facility, or an intermediate-care facility for up to five days in each instance. This is a limited benefit that can only be used occasionally, and the number of respite days cannot exceed twenty percent of the total hospice days. The patient will receive the same type of care as he would if he were in the home. This means that the hospital or facility will not implement curative treatment and will not subject the patient to additional testing or monitoring such as X-rays or laboratory tests. Inpatient respite care is covered by Medicare *only* if it is arranged by the hospice team, and you may be responsible for a co-pay.[22]

If you or your loved one meets enrollment criteria for hospice, it is important to know what hospice does and does not cover under Medicare.

Hospice Services Covered by Medicare

The following services are covered:

- doctor services
- nursing care
- medical equipment such as a wheelchair, hospital bed, or oxygen
- medical supplies such as bandages and catheters
- prescription drugs for symptom control or pain relief
- hospice aide and homemaker services
- physical and occupational therapy if the therapy is to improve symptoms and not curative

- speech therapy for symptom management
- social-work services
- dietary counseling
- grief and loss counseling for you and your family
- short-term inpatient care for pain and symptom management only if arranged by your hospice team
- short-term respite care only if arranged by your hospice team
- any other Medicare-covered services needed to manage your pain and other symptoms related to your terminal illness as recommended by your hospice team

What hospice services are not covered by Medicare? The following services are *not* covered:

- treatment intended to cure your terminal illness
- prescription drugs to cure your terminal illness
- care from any hospice provider that wasn't set up by the hospice medical team
- room and board (Medicare does not pay for room and board when you have hospice care in your home or another facility where you live, such as a nursing home. If you have Medicare as well as Medicaid, Medicaid will pay for room and board and Medicare will pay for the hospice services).
- care in an emergency room, inpatient facility care, or ambulance transportation, unless it is arranged by your hospice team or is unrelated to your terminal illness[23]

What are the costs for hospice care that is covered by Medicare? As of 2013 your costs would consist of the following, though this may change in the future:[24]

- There is no charge for hospice care. Hospice benefits are paid directly to the hospice provider on a *per diem* basis.
- Prescription drugs may require a co-payment of no more than five dollars for each prescription.
- You will need to pay 5 percent of the Medicare-approved amount for inpatient respite care.

Barriers to Hospice

Despite the potential benefits of hospice, multiple barriers to hospice care have been identified. They include the following situations:

- There has been a lack of advance care planning, including failure to complete an advance directive or Durable Power of Attorney for Healthcare. A 2011 survey conducted in the UK and Ireland showed that 69 and 78 percent of respondents respectively had not talked to anybody about their wishes for end-of-life treatment. A study in 2008 found that older adults often trust or prefer others to make end-of-life decisions for them, but even when they trusted someone (which was most often children rather than a spouse), less than half had spoken with the person they expected to make decisions for them.
- Older adults believe they need to shield their adult children from the eventuality of their death.
- Older adults trust in others such as God, their family, and their physician to make end-of-life decisions for them.

- Their preferences are unknown. This includes those older adults who do not know what their preferences are for end-of-life care.
- The family is rarely together. This was identified by older adults as well as younger adults as an impediment to discussing end-of-life preferences.
- Fear of death was cited as a reason for avoiding discussing death.
- The most frequent reason older adults give for not having completed an advance directive or Durable Power of Attorney for Healthcare was they felt they were "too healthy" and reported they did not want to think about illness and dying.
- People may not be able to hear information given to them regarding their health or terminal disease, and therefore denial prohibits them from being able to act upon the information.
- The physician wants to continue curative care.
- The physician feels discomfort discussing a terminal diagnosis and prognosis. Physicians often express a better prognosis to the patient than they believe is the truth. Physicians have reported that even when patients ask specifically for a prognosis, they only give frank estimates 37 percent of the time for fear of causing the patient to lose hope.
- The physician lacks knowledge regarding hospice services and benefits.
- The physician fails to discuss hospice as an option.
- The physician is reluctant to lose control or contact with the patient.
- Family caregivers reported never being told the patient's illness could not be cured. Of those who were told they

had a terminal illness, 40 percent were never given a life expectancy.

- The patient or family desires to continue curative care.
- The patient or family lacks knowledge about hospice.
- The family is unable to provide full-time caregiving.
- The patient or family mistrusts the medical care system. African Americans are more likely than whites to view hospice as "giving up."
- The hospice system itself causes barriers. For example, there may be a lack of racial diversity of hospice staff.
- Hospice care may be geographically inaccessible to patients. Less populated or rural areas may not have the availability of hospice due to geographic isolation.

There are also racial and ethnic disparities in the use of hospice. Korean Americans and Mexican Americans are significantly less likely to believe that patients should be told a terminal diagnosis or to make decisions about using life support. The Navajo culture views medical information as harmful. In Taiwan, neither Western-oriented nor traditional Chinese doctors give information related to diagnosis and prognosis to patients who have a life-threatening illness; instead, this information is given to family members, who in turn inform the patient.

Hispanic Americans and African Americans are more likely than non-Hispanic whites to want their doctors to keep them alive regardless of how ill they are. African Americans are less likely than whites to have an advance directive and are more likely to prefer life-sustaining treatment, even when it is known the treatment is futile. This may be related to a lack of trust in the healthcare system given the legacy of slavery, abuses in medical experimentation, economic and legal injustices, and racial profiling.

I live in an area with several large Amish communities. Decisions regarding healthcare are decided by the church elders or bishops in the community, and the patient undergoes whatever treatment is decided upon. Patients do not have any input into what treatment they will receive. The Amish often consult their local herbalist, chiropractor, reflexologist, Brauche practitioner (one who uses words, charms and physical manipulation to treat illness) before consulting the western medical community. The Amish see expensive life-prolonging treatment as excessive and unjustified in those diagnosed with a terminal illness and often elect to let the patient die with dignity.[25]

The Timing of Enrollment in Hospice

In order to receive hospice care, the patient's physician must certify that the patient has a life expectancy of six months or less. In the case of patients with a cancer diagnosis, it is relatively easy for the physician to project the trajectory of the disease process. The pattern of rapid functional decline that occurs in the last three months of life for most cancer patients is generally recognized by patients and healthcare providers as the beginning of the dying process.[26] However, it is difficult to determine life expectancy for the elderly population who do not have a diagnosis of cancer but are living with two or more chronic diseases with periods of stability interspersed with acute exacerbations for years or even decades. It is difficult to know whether the patient will respond to treatment for an acute exacerbation or whether, despite treatment, his condition will continue to deteriorate. In 2012 those age 85 years and older represented the largest percentage of patients receiving hospice care at 40.5 percent, and these are those patients who had been living with multiple chronic diseases for years.[27]

Referral to and enrollment in hospice may not occur until the patient's condition is quickly nearing the end-of-life, and therefore he or she may not receive hospice services at all or may not receive hospice long enough to realize the full benefit of what hospice has to offer for the patient and the family.

The point at which a terminally ill patient enters hospice can have a major influence on the nature and amount of physical and psychological suffering the patient and the patient's family endure. There have been multiple studies that have surveyed the families of patients in hospice regarding the optimal time for referral to hospice, and the results vary. What may seem just right to one family may seem too soon or too late to another. Family caregivers who thought the referral to hospice occurred too late reported more unmet needs for the patient and family. The unmet needs for the patient were reported as inadequate pain management, shortness of breath, and emotional support. Unmet needs for the family were reported as lack of emotional support and feeling less prepared for what to expect during the dying process and how to manage patient symptoms.[28]

Many experts recommend hospice care for at least three months, with a minimum of thirty days in order for the patient and family to receive the maximum benefit hospice has to offer.[29] Despite this, in 2012 the median length of time in hospice was 18.7 days. Half of all hospice patients received care for less than three weeks, and half received care for more than three weeks. Approximately 35.5 percent died or were discharged within seven days of admission to hospice.[30] These numbers demonstrate that we need to do a better job at initiating end-of-life discussions in order to serve patients and families more effectively. Because of the barriers listed above that prevent physicians from initiating hospice discussions, the patient or the family may need to initiate this discussion with their physician or healthcare providers. The optimal time for this discussion is in the outpatient setting before the patient requires hospice. This helps prevent decisions from having to be made during a time of crisis and also ensures the patient's wishes will be honored at the right time.

Conclusion

By accepting death and dying as a natural process, the need for palliative care and hospice care will increase over the next twenty to thirty years as the population continues to age. In the United States 78 million "baby boomers" are now entering the phase of life associated with the peak incidence of cancer, heart disease, and other life-threatening and chronic diseases.[31] By recognizing the natural process of death and dying and by encouraging open discussions with patients and families, we will be able to establish a trusting relationship that not only provides treatment that is consistent with patients' values and life goals but also reduces isolation and fear as they enter the last phase of their mortal life.

CHAPTER 8

FAMILY DYNAMICS

There is an interconnectedness among members that bonds the family, much like mountain climbers who rope themselves together when climbing a mountain, so that if someone would slip or need support, he's held up by the others until he regains his footing.
—Phil McGraw, *Family First*

While working with patients and families for over 35 years, I have noticed that although each family is unique, there are similarities in how families and friends respond to and cope with the illness of someone that is important to them, whether the patient is experiencing an acute illness which may be life threatening or an exacerbation of a chronic disease. The response of those around the patient can range from helpful and productive to pathological and hurtful. They may respond in a way that is disruptive and possibly endangers the patient's health or safety.

The illness of someone close to us can be a reminder of our own frailty and mortality and therefore can be difficult for some people to cope with. I once knew a couple who severed their friendship with a mutual friend of many years because he was in declining health and becoming quite frail. He wasn't "fun" anymore, and they didn't want to waste their time with someone who wasn't "fun." When he died, they didn't even bother to extend their sympathies to his widow. They said they couldn't be bothered. I thought they were being extremely selfish and immature and at first this response angered me, but I came to realize it may have been the only way they knew how to cope with the illness and eventual loss of a friend. By severing their friendship they were able to spare themselves the emotional pain of losing a friend, and this also saved them from having to acknowledge their own mortality.

Each family member learns where or how they fit within and outside the family and acts accordingly. Certain family members take more prominent roles and provide leadership, while other family members "go with the flow" and tag along for the ride, expressing few opinions and leaving all decision making to others. Other family members become estranged and interact with the family only when it is demanded of them. These roles are deeply ingrained. Behaviors are learned and honed over the years.

The following are common roles that exist within a family:

- The matriarch or patriarch may rule the household and the children even after they are grown and living on their own. This role can vary by ethnicity or other factors such as an absent parent, or when one is just more domineering than the other. Some families are ruled "with an iron fist" and others are more egalitarian.
- The oldest child is often held to high standards by the parents and is often expected to set an example or fulfill a leadership role to the younger children even when they are adults. This may be a role the oldest child accepts or rebels against.
- The youngest child may be the most immature. He or she may have been "babied" all his or her life, and therefore expectations are low. He or she is not expected to make decisions.

- The rebel does not conform to the standards of the family and generally takes an opposite stand against all others in the family. The rebel often feels as though he has been short changed in some way throughout his or her life.

- The know-it-all is an expert in all things within and outside the family. He or she dismisses the opinions and knowledge of others as wrong if they differ from his or her own. The know-it-all often talks or shouts over others in the family in order to get his or her own way.

- Self-centered family members are only interested in how the illness of another affects them personally. They are unable to put themselves in the place of the patient and see events from the patient's perspective.

- Dependent family members need someone to take care of them. This may be in the form of physical care or simply in the form of someone telling them what to do. Dependent family members rarely express an opinion of their own.

- Estranged family members only interact with the family during times of crisis such as a life-threatening illness of a family member or themselves. They are often angry at the patient or other family members for some perceived slight that may or may not have happened.

- 'Too busy' family members put their job, children, or personal needs ahead of the needs of an ill elder family member. They usually live out of town and are therefore not able to help care for the ill family member, but they are not at a loss in expressing what others should be doing and criticizing them when they don't live up to their expectations.

How a family reacts to any kind of stress sets the stage for how they will react when an elder family member is faced with a terminal illness. All of these individuals play an integral role in the terminally ill elder's response to his or her illness and subsequent decisions made regarding healthcare and treatment. The stress of having to interact with the healthcare team can influence the patient as well as the family members in how they are able to accept and comprehend information and in how they respond to that information. This dynamic can change over time as the patient goes from having chronic illnesses that are manageable to an end-of-life scenario or is diagnosed with a terminal illness.

A terminal illness forces an intimate relationship between the patient, the family, and the healthcare team. The patient and family are asked to trust the healthcare team in this stressful time, and this may be too much for them. Some families never develop trust in the healthcare team, and this sets up an environment that makes caring for the patient difficult. I encountered a woman, M.B., with multiple chronic complex medical and physical needs. Her son was her primary caregiver and had been for a long time. Each time she was hospitalized he would blame all her problems on the home health agency that helped care for her. He did not trust anyone when it came to the care of his mother. Over the years he had fired multiple home health agencies and caregivers. He had alienated all of his siblings and other family members by his behavior and general mistrust of everyone.

When I talked with him over the course of several hospitalizations, he would often become enraged and yell at the nurses and social worker whenever they tried to discuss his mother's condition and care. It became evident that the patient's son could not accept his mother's illness and poor prognosis and therefore blamed everyone else for "causing her problems."

The family may respond to a loved one's illness as a cohesive unit or as separate individuals within or outside of the family unit.

There are family members who make the obligatory visit to the patient while they are in the hospital and then they leave and are never heard from again. Sometimes the family may remain on the scene and participate in the care of the patient, but they may be angry at the patient for becoming ill or argue with the patient regarding his or her treatment decisions.

Of course, there are those families who are close and have a good relationship and are very supportive without being overbearing or critical. They are there for the patient physically as well as emotionally. They are supportive of the patient making his or her own healthcare decisions when he or she is able, and they are respectful of the patient's requests. They have knowledge of the patient's wishes and use the advance directive or defer to the Durable Power of Attorney for Healthcare to make decisions which they know will be in line with the patient's wishes. These families are a delight to work with and warm my heart.

Often a person becomes incapacitated enough that they are no longer able to adequately care for themselves but can remain in the home with the proper care and supervision. This is often the case with those who have dementia, heart failure, COPD, diabetes, or other chronic diseases that may not be immediately life threatening but require twenty-four hour supervision to ensure the patient is cared for adequately and is not placed in danger by remaining in the home.

Caring for someone in their home can seem a daunting task and is not for everyone. However, for those who are able and willing to care for an elderly relative in the home, it can be a rewarding experience for both the patient and the caregiver(s). There are many resources in the community that can help in the home. Agencies such as home health, the Division of Aging, Meals on Wheels, church groups, and Hospice are available. Certain agencies, such as home health, require a physician's order for their services, and these may be provided on a limited basis depending on the patient's needs and insurance coverage.

Social workers are invaluable sources of information regarding resources in the community. They can help with contacting agencies, as well as informing you which services are provided and covered by insurance and which services are not covered by insurance and are an out-of-pocket expense.

When caring for an elderly family member, you may not initially need help from agencies, but as the patient's condition deteriorates over time and their care needs escalate, you may find you are no longer able to manage on your own, and this will be the time to elicit help from others. It can be difficult for the caregiver to admit he or she needs help, as this can be a clear sign that their loved one is declining despite all their efforts, and the caregiver may feel as if he or she has failed the loved one in some way.

Some caregivers become so involved in their caring role that they become isolated and lose contact with other members of the family and friends who may be able to help. Although it may be difficult, it is important to stay in touch with those important to you and the patient. It is important to ask for and accept help when needed. It doesn't mean you haven't done a good job caring for your loved one. It just means you need help to take care of yourself as well as your loved one.

I have categorized family caregiving roles into eight groups and describe them further below:

- the spouse as sole caregiver
- the family unit as caregiver
- the individual family member as caregiver
- the institution as caregiver
- the moocher
- the family in denial

- the duck
- the grudge holder

The Spouse as Sole Caregiver

With our mobile society many families are living apart. Generations are separated by miles. Often parents may live in one city while children and grandchildren live in another city, another state, or even another country. This situation often leads to the elderly couple being left to cope with burgeoning health issues alone. When one spouse becomes incapacitated to the point of needing twenty-four hour care, their spouse often takes on this task alone, as family is not near and is unable to help, or if they are near, they may not be available due to work and family responsibilities of their own. The elderly parents may not feel comfortable asking for help. I have found elderly parents are not always truthful with their out-of-town children about the condition of their spouse or their own ability to cope and provide the needed care. They often don't want to alarm or worry the children. They also do not want to appear needy or incompetent in caring for their spouse. I am often told, "They're so busy. I don't want to bother them" or "What can they do? They live so far away." There is also the concern that if the children find out the severity of the situation, they will want to place the ill parent in a nursing home. Although this is usually a well-meaning suggestion to diminish the burden on the caregiving spouse, it is a dreadful idea to many and one to be avoided if at all possible.

As this book focuses on care of the elderly, we must realize that the spouses of the elderly are often elderly themselves and often have their own chronic diseases they are living with and trying to manage. I have noticed that it is rare for an elderly couple to have the same level of functioning. Usually one spouse has an incapacitating chronic disease, while the other is relatively healthy with few health issues of his or her own.

Spouses who are sole caregivers are committed to caring for their spouse and keeping them in the home as long as possible. Often they have made promises to never place them in a nursing home but to keep them at home and care for them until they pass away. Although these spouses are well meaning and are willing to take on the responsibility of sole caregiver, this is an arrangement that can continue only as long as the caregivers are able to adequately rest and care for themselves as well as the patient. The caregivers often feel as if they have failed somehow if the patient becomes sick or needs hospitalization.

When sole caregivers become ill and are unable to continue providing care for their spouse, this often represents a crisis for the couple. It may lead to feelings of guilt on the part of the sole caregivers as they are now ill and cannot care for their spouse. They may also have significant anxiety, not for themselves, but for their spouse, as they don't know what's going to happen to them if they cannot continue to care for them.

In other marriages, patients may make their spouses feel guilty if they say they cannot care for them due to their own physical limitations or health conditions. These patients often refuse to go to a nursing home or long-term care facility, demanding instead that their spouse take care of them. They often refuse outside help as well. This is a dysfunctional relationship and leads to the spouse becoming completely exhausted physically as well as emotionally. The caregiver may become ill and require hospitalization due to the demands of caring for the ill spouse.

In the case of the elderly with significant dementia, the patient's physical needs may be relatively easy to meet initially, but as the dementia progresses and the patient becomes more dependent for his or her everyday needs, including eating, toileting, bathing, and dressing, the caregiver may become exhausted. Behavioral problems such as anger, agitation, and wandering, particularly at night, may develop, which leads to poor sleep and exhaustion for the caregiver. I once met a couple where the husband had advanced dementia. He slept very little day or night and wandered at night. The wife reported she had to move the living room sofa in front of the front door every night, and this is where she slept with "one eye open" to prevent her husband from leaving the house and wandering away. She eventually required hospitalization to treat her own exhaustion and chronic illnesses, which she had neglected in order to care for her husband. Her husband was placed in a nursing home at that time. The wife experienced terrible guilt for "letting my husband down."

The older couple may refuse outside help because they do not want strangers in their home or because they believe it is their duty and responsibility to care for their spouse no matter what. This may be an unrealistic expectation depending on the needs of the patient. I have met petite women barely weighing one hundred pounds who were trying to care for husbands who were much bigger and significantly outweighed them. One woman's husband weighed 300 pounds, and she was trying to care for him all by herself because this is what her husband demanded. They will try to lift them into wheelchairs or turn them in bed, and this invariably leads to injury to the caregiver, the patient, or both. Regardless of the dedication of such women, they are physically not up to the demands of caring for someone much larger than themselves.

I have met many children of elderly parents who came into town to find a situation that to them was appalling. Both the patient and the caregiver may be losing weight from skipping meals, because the caregiver cannot get to the grocery store and there isn't adequate food in the home. They may not be taking their medications properly. The house may be disorganized and dirty due to lack of time or energy to wash the dishes, do the laundry, or keep up with the housekeeping. The caregiver may have been ill but continues to try to care for the spouse. To find the parents in such dire straits is shocking, especially if the children had been led to believe that all was well and the parents were fine.

This is a time of crisis for the family, the caregiver, and the patient. What can we do to support and help the sole caregiver? First, the most important thing children can do for their parents as they age is to stay connected and involved. As family members, we need to be involved in our elderly parents' lives in order to ensure the information we are receiving from the caregiver is accurate. This can be difficult when we are separated by miles. It is easy in our busy lives to believe everything is okay. A trip home for a few days can be very enlightening about just what the needs of the patient and the difficulties and challenges of the caregiver are. We can encourage the sole caregiver to accept help in the home to relieve him or her of some of the duties or to obtain equipment that will help care for the patient. This may be in the form of nurses, nurse's aides, or housekeeping services. Equipment such as lifts and bedside commodes can help prevent falls and injuries. Just having someone to help with the bathing or laundry can be extremely helpful, or someone to stay with the patient while the spouse goes shopping. A social worker can be invaluable in helping sort through all the issues and setting up services and equipment as needed in the home.

The Family as Caregiver

The spouse may not be able to be a caregiver. The patient may be widowed, divorced, or single and must rely on family members such as children, nieces and nephews, and grandchildren for care. This additional help may be difficult to accept in the beginning, but often the spouse or patient comes to realize they are dependent on others in order to be able to stay in their home. Studies have shown that the majority of people want to stay in their own home, and indeed this is the experience I have had.

The very idea of going to a facility of some type, whether it is an assisted-living facility or a nursing home, is often rejected at the first mention, and the elderly person refuses to discuss it. Every elderly person fears having to go to a nursing home. They often equate this with death. "That's where people go to die" is what I have been told repeatedly over the years. In an effort to keep patients in their own home and out of institutions such as nursing homes, families pitch in and work together to provide twenty-four hour supervision and care. This is often done in shifts, and one person acts as coordinator to ensure adequate coverage. This arrangement ensures the patient receives the companionship and physical care they require and provides for proper monitoring of medication administration and effectiveness and proper nutrition through regular meal preparation.

These patients tend to do well and know their family loves them. The family as a whole tends to do well, as the burden of caregiving is shared. This prevents burnout of one caregiver and also gives family members time to work and spend time with their own families.

The family as caregiver requires a fair amount of coordination and communication among the family members, and one person should be designated as coordinator to ensure there aren't any lapses in caregiver coverage. This arrangement may be supplemented with volunteer and paid help. The paid employee may provide services the family members are not comfortable with, such as bathing and personal care. However, non-licensed caregivers, such as patient-care technicians and companions, may not be covered by insurance, and paying them is often an out-of-pocket expense that can be a limiting factor for some families based on financial resources.

Families often enlist the help of neighbors, friends, volunteers, or church members to provide companionship to the patient. They may also enlist their help in running errands or meal preparation. These are small tasks that are easy to do and do not require a lot of time or commitment, but they are very helpful to the family. It is important to enlist the help of as many people as possible in order to avoid caregiver fatigue and burnout. It also helps the patient to feel connected to family, friends, and the community.

Insurance may cover services provided by licensed professionals such as registered nurses (RN), licensed practical/vocational nurses (LPN/LVN), physical therapists (PT), occupational therapists (OT), and speech therapists (ST). However, the frequency and number of visits and services that are covered will vary depending on the insurance coverage.

I have encountered many families who have successfully taken care of a loved one in the home for years and thus avoided institutional care. This close involvement of family leads to early identification of changes in the patient's health so that these issues can be addressed quickly, often avoiding hospitalization.

Patients who are cared for in their home often express gratitude for the care and attention they receive from their family and appreciate the efforts of their family in keeping them out of a nursing home. The family members experience gratification and fulfillment in their role as caregivers. They feel good about the care they have provided and their willingness and ability to keep the patient at home and out of a nursing home.

Caring for a family member in the home often leads to open discussions regarding end-of-life wishes. This provides the family with first-hand knowledge of all the health issues the patient is dealing with and also seems to provide the family with realistic expectations of what the patient is capable of in terms of self-care and prognosis. Family caregivers often have a closer relationship with the patient's physician or healthcare provider. This offers the opportunity for dialogue over time as the patient's condition changes to ensure the care of the patient remains consistent with his or her wishes. Family caregivers also have an acceptance of the patient's death when the time comes, as they know they have done all they could for the patient.

The Individual Family Member as Caregiver

When the family as a whole is unable to provide care, a single family member such as a child, grandchild, niece, or nephew frequently becomes the caregiver. This situation may occur by default. The family as a whole recognizes that the patient requires care and would like for him or her to remain in the home as long as possible, but only one person is willing to step up and take on the responsibility of being a full-time caregiver. This person may have to give up their job in order to become a full-time caregiver. He or she often moves into the elderly person's home or goes to the home multiple times a day. They may hire in help and elicit the help of volunteers, church members, and friends as well.

When an individual becomes sole caregiver, this is a relief to all other family members. Some family members will take this as a signal that they do not need to be involved and do not need to worry about their elder family member, because now someone else is taking care of him or her. Others will stay involved to varying degrees. This may include help on a routine basis or an occasional basis. There are those who never participate in the care of the elder, yet this does not inhibit them from telling the caregiver how they think he or she should be caring for the elder or what they think he or she is doing wrong. A situation like this is terribly difficult for the caregiver, who often feels isolated, abused, and taken advantage of by siblings or other family members and can become resentful toward them and the patient.

What can you do? Stay involved. Have the individual caregiver assign you tasks that you can do. These may include running errands, cooking, cleaning, researching resources, or just providing a break for the caregiver. We all need downtime to reenergize ourselves and to address our own needs, such as getting a haircut, paying bills, or visiting with friends, even if it is just for one day. This will help the caregiver from experiencing burnout from the responsibility of caring for an ill elderly family member. The caregiver and the patient will appreciate your help.

The Institution as Caregiver

There are many reasons why patients require care in an institution rather than in their home. They may be too weak to return home immediately after hospitalization or may require continued care to optimize their functional capacity and ability to care for themselves. It may be that they do not have any family available or anyone who is capable of caring for them. The patient's care needs may exceed the ability of the family to care for him or her. The patient may already reside in a long-term care facility. Some families do not want the responsibility of caring for someone.

Even though they stay involved and visit the patient frequently, they are not comfortable providing the actual physical care the patient requires. There are many other reasons as well.

Some patients may need a short stay in an institution such as a rehabilitation (rehab) facility following an accident, hospitalization, or surgery, or perhaps they may need a short stay in a skilled nursing facility (SNF) if they are not able to meet admission criteria to a rehab facility. These admissions are intended to be short in duration and restore the patient to his or her prior level or an improved level of functioning with the goal of returning home.

Admission to a long-term acute-care (LTAC) hospital may be needed if the patient has complex medical needs which cannot be handled in the home, for example complex wound care, ventilator weaning, or IV antibiotics. As the name suggests, long-term acute-care hospitals are hospitals with a minimum length of stay of approximately twenty days. The focus of care is restorative. These facilities provide care to patients who are too ill to be cared for in a rehab or SNF. The goal is either to discharge patients to rehab, SNF, or home or to transition them to a long-term care facility (nursing home) depending on their progress and care needs.

Placement in a long-term care facility (nursing home) is needed when the patient's needs exceeds the ability of others to care for him or her in the home. This is often accompanied by feelings of guilt on the part of the family or significant other, particularly if there were promises made in the past that they would never put them in a nursing home. Long-term placement is often the "end of the road" for many families who have cared for the patient at home, but the patient's care needs exhaust the families physically, emotionally, or financially.

Often placement in a nursing home occurs when the patient has severe dementia and therefore is unaware of his or her surroundings. At this point the family feels the patient will not know the difference of who their caregiver is.

In some smaller communities the nursing home is seen as "not so bad," as the patients and families know the people who work there, and some of their friends are there, so they will be able to see their friends and stay connected with the community. This definitely places a positive spin on their need for long-term placement. It is always preferable to find a facility that is close to family so that they are able to visit and continue to be involved in the patient's life.

Even if your family member goes to a nursing home, stay involved. Visit or call as frequently as you can to ensure he or she is receiving the proper care. Frequent visits can help identify changes in your loved one's health that the staff may not recognize. It takes time for the staff at the nursing home to get to know your loved one and be able to recognize when something has changed. Talking to the staff about your loved one's food preferences and regular routine can help the staff establish a schedule that considers his or her individual needs. This will also help him or her adjust to new surroundings, ward off the onset of depression, and realize he or she has not been abandoned by family.

The Moocher

This can be a sticky situation. The Moocher is a family member, often an adult child or grandchild, who moves in with the elder and takes on the responsibility of "caring" for the elder. This is a situation where the relative moves in with the elder in order to meet his or her own needs and not the needs of the elder. Unfortunately, this is not uncommon, and I have met many patients over the years in this situation. When I use the word "caring," I use it loosely, as these family members really aren't caring for the patient at all. They are living with the patient in order to have a place to live and access to the patient's property such as their car, narcotic pain medications, and financial assets.

These family members do not have any means of supporting themselves and may be involved in illegal activity. Since they are living with their relative, a "what's yours is mine" mentality arises, and the "caregiver" takes advantage of the elder. Some patients have told me they are afraid of their family member and feel powerless to do anything about it as they are at the mercy of the family member and worry that reporting the situation will only make matters worse.

I have met patients in uncontrollable pain because their "caregiver" either stole and consumed the patient's pain medications or sold them on the street for money. Other family members will express their concern that the elder is not being cared for properly or is being taken advantage of, but they too feel powerless to do anything about the situation. This is a form of elder abuse and must be reported to the agency in your particular state that handles such investigations. You can make an anonymous report via telephone. In Missouri, where I live, this is the Missouri Department of Health & Senior Services, often called "Adult Protective Services" in other states. If the patient is in the hospital, you can ask to speak with a social worker, who is by law a mandated reporter and will get involved once the situation is brought to his or her attention.

Mrs. S.L. was a 79-year-old woman who suffered from advanced dementia, and her son was her caregiver. Mrs. S.L. had sustained a fall which resulted in a hip fracture. Her son reported to the social worker that he left her lying on the floor all night because she was crying and yelling and this annoyed him so he went to bed. He called an ambulance the following morning, and she was brought to the hospital. She not only had a hip fracture but was emaciated and filthy from lack of regular meals and basic care. It appeared as if she hadn't had a bath in a long time. When informed that he would be reported for elder abuse and that Mrs. S.L. would be placed in a nursing home at discharge, the son's only concern was what he was going to do for money since he was using his mother's Social Security check to live on and he would no longer have access to it. He showed no concern for his mother, only for himself. This was a terribly unfortunate but not uncommon situation.

The Family in Denial

There are two situations that I have found that lead to a family's inability to accept the illness of a family member. First, I have met several children of elderly patients over the years who believed the patient was faking their illness in order to get attention. I have encountered people who either exaggerated an illness or faked it altogether in order to get attention. This behavior is synonymous with the boy who cried wolf. Patients may seek attention from their spouse or significant other, the healthcare system, their school, their family, or whomever by exaggerating their health problems or by completely fabricating an illness. By doing this they receive the attention they are seeking, even if the attention is negative. This behavior keeps the patient from having to deal with responsibilities such as work, child rearing, managing finances, or whatever it may be the patient is trying to avoid.

This behavior may have been a pattern in these patients' lives for years, and therefore, when they do become ill, no one believes them. The family is often emotionally exhausted and angry with them for their prior deceptions and therefore do not respond to them when they *are* sick. They may ignore physical signs of illness. It can be a challenge to convince the family that the patient is truly ill and may have a life-threatening condition. When they finally accept the patient's illness, they often become angry with the patient and may abandon the patient physically as well as emotionally. The family relationship may become even more strained. The family may express that the patient deserves to be sick because of his or her past behavior and that they do not want any part in caring for the patient. These patients are often placed in a long-term care facility since the family is unwilling to care for them. What can be done in these situations? I encourage counseling for the patient (if able) and the family to help them deal with their emotions.

The second scenario that may affect the patient's family's ability to accept the the an end-of-life terminal diagnosis is when a patient has been living with chronic medical diseases such as COPD, heart disease, lymphoma, or diabetes for years or even decades. Throughout the years the patient may have had multiple acute exacerbations of his or her chronic diseases that could be treated and the patient may have rallied.

Even if the patient has had a steady decline in health and functioning over the years, the family expects him or her to pull through as he or she has in the past. When confronted with the inability to "pull the patient back" from yet another acute exacerbation, the family often responds with confusion, such as "He's always gotten better before." This is often the case with patients who have been successful in staying active and who often minimize their illness to their family out of concern that they don't want to worry them. It may take multiple conversations with the family to help them to understand the severity of the situation and therefore help them to be available to support the patient and provide care if needed during this time. It may also be the time to recommend hospice care to the patient and family.

The Duck

The Duck is the family member who lives out of state, flies into town when an elderly family member is hospitalized, shits on everyone and everything, and then flies out of town back to where they came from never to be seen or heard from again until the next health crisis or hospitalization. The Duck does not have any caregiving responsibilities and only limited contact with the patient over extended periods of time. It may be months to years since the Duck last saw the patient. These are the relatives who rely on other members of the family to provide all the care while remaining blissfully ignorant of the needs of the patient and the amount of care the patient requires. They may have occasional telephone calls with the caregiver or patient, but they really do not have any idea of the patient's physical or medical conditions, and they don't want to know. When the caregiver tries to enlist their help in caring for their family member, they are always too busy and tend to deny the severity of the patient's condition. However, they are never at a loss for giving the caregiver their opinion as to what they should or should not be doing. They are very generous with their opinions and criticism.

When the patient is hospitalized, often in the end stages of life, the Duck will fly into town and find extreme fault with the caregiver for whatever he or she has or has not done. "If they had taken better care of him, then he wouldn't be in this condition in the first place!" They contradict both the caregiver and the patient. They try to take over decision making from the patient and the caregiver. They ignore or override the patient's requests and the healthcare team's recommendations. They refuse to acknowledge the advance directive and Durable Power of Attorney for Healthcare, and they demand unreasonable and often futile care for the patient, often ignoring the patient's protests. Then they fly out of town back to where they came from, leaving a trail of hard feelings, tears, and frustration, having contributed nothing positive to helping the caregiver or the patient. They often demand that the caregiver "do more" for the patient without regard to what "do more" means or if it is even possible to do more. The patient may not want the caregiver or anyone else to do more for him. He may be ready for hospice.

I believe the Duck behaves this way out of guilt about not being involved in the patient's life. It is much easier to criticize others rather than yourself, and it is certainly easier than having to actually participate in caring for the person. As long as someone else is taking on the responsibility of caring for the patient, then the Duck doesn't have to. This does not keep them from finding fault, nor does this keep them from making a mess of things when they do show up.

If you are an out-of-town relative, do not presume you know what is best for the patient. Unless you want to be the full-time caregiver, you must trust and have faith in the one who *is* the caregiver. He or she may not be doing things exactly as you would, but then again, you are not there and you're not doing anything. Respect the advance directive and Durable Power of Attorney as the legal documents they are.

Don't be a Duck.

The Grudge Holder

Dysfunctional families with long-standing arguments or grudges who do not have good coping skills or interrelationships become even more dysfunctional when a family member is facing a terminal illness. This situation can lead to severe conflict between the patient and members of the family, and it is quite challenging for the healthcare team as well as the patient. It can shift the focus from the needs of the patient to the needs of the family.

The Grudge Holder are those family members who have unresolved issues with the patient or other family members. They are capable of holding a grudge for years. This often leads to a degree of estrangement between the Grudge Holder and the patient and family. Reasons for a grudge are as varied as the people who hold them, but they often involve a perceived slight or favoritism toward another family member (often a sibling) over them. The grudge may be due to financial issues.

Often when an elderly person remarries after the death of a spouse, problems arise with adult children accepting the new spouse. Often a grudge is motivated by concerns over money and what they may or may not inherit when the parent dies. My experience has been that Grudge Holders feel as if the patient or family owes them a certain amount of money, property, or other assets. In the rural area where I live, this often involves disputes over farm land and other real estate.

The Grudge Holder often has little to no contact with the patient until they become ill and then he or she swoops in and wants to take control of the situation. Grudge Holders are looking for what is "rightfully theirs," and they attempt to bully the patient or family into giving it to them. They may also want "everything" done regardless of how futile it may be so that they can have more time with the patient in order to try to influence the patient into giving them what they feel they have been denied. This is terribly dysfunctional and disruptive, and it is certainly not in the best interest of the patient. The patient and family often look to the healthcare team, the social worker in particular, to help diffuse this situation. Although the social worker can help with family communication, years of family dysfunction cannot be resolved by the social worker in one or two days. If the Grudge Holder hasn't spoken to his or her brother in twenty years, don't expect the social worker to make them best friends.

The focus with the Grudge Holder is the same as with anyone else—on the patient and what is best for the patient. Unfortunately, this can be very difficult if not impossible for Grudge Holders to comprehend, after all it's all about them, or so they think.

The hospital or the patient's bedside is *not* the place for family grievances or grudges. Keep them to yourself. Everybody already knows what they are anyway.

CHAPTER 9

CONCLUSION

Do not seek death. Death will find you. But seek the road which makes death a fulfillment.
—Dag Hammarskjold

To contemplate one's mortality can be a frightening prospect. Throughout our lives we experience the death of others, but somehow we believe we will be spared the inevitable. The mere idea of growing old is pushed to the recesses of our mind. My mother, who is eighty-four, cannot believe she has become old. She tells me, "I never thought it would happen to me." My father had the same amazement as he watched his children become older and grow into their fifties. It was hard for him to admit that he was becoming older too. Middle age has been pushed back from forty to fifty. We believe we are young even when there is evidence to the contrary, and the years march on with the celebration of each birthday, more candles on the cake symbolizing our aging.

In order to be able to have a good death, we must determine for ourselves what a good death is. Will you "fight to the death," or will you acquiesce and "let nature take its course?" Will you yield to the wants and desires of others, or will you choose your own path and embrace it? We must all find the path we are comfortable with, the path that meets our physical, emotional, psychological, spiritual, and social needs.

This book has attempted to provide a practical guide for taking the steps toward addressing medical treatment in general and end-of-life treatment, specifically in order to ensure you remain in control of your healthcare decisions throughout your life and death.

Regardless of what path is chosen, we need to fully explore all of our treatment options, which include state-of-the-art extensive treatment, withholding treatment, withdrawing treatment, palliative care, and hospice care. We must consider which of these options best meets our needs and then share our plans with those who are most important to us. We need to recognize that our needs may change as we are faced with acute and chronic diseases. What may have been desired or considered the best treatment at one time may change, and we must be able to evaluate our needs and communicate them clearly to our family, friends, and physician.

We must also realize that we may not always be in full command of our capacities and that we may need someone to help us along our journey. Completing an advance directive and Durable Power of Attorney for Healthcare can ensure that we continue to have a voice through the legal written word at a time we are unable to express ourselves in other ways.

Although it is a hard topic to bring up, and no one wants to think about dying, it is a conversation we must have in order to ensure we have our own good death. Ellen Goodman, a Pulitzer Prize-winning columnist, co-founded the Conversation Project to have "the Conversation" in response to her own mother's fight with dementia, which left Ms. Goodman in the position of making healthcare decisions for her mother without ever having discussed her end-of-life wishes.

There are also Death Cafés springing up across the globe, where people gather to have coffee and cake and talk about end-of-life issues. These are non-threatening gatherings in communities to give you an opportunity to learn about advance directives and Durable Powers of Attorney for Healthcare and to have your questions answered. They are also a way to meet others who are seeking answers to the same questions as you. These forums are not just for the elderly but for anyone of any age who wishes to attend. There have been 775 Death Cafés held in eighteen countries as of this writing.

To find additional information about Death Cafés in your area, search for Death Cafés on the internet. For additional information regarding the Conversation Project, as well as a helpful starter kit and guide on how to start the conversation with your family go to theconversationproject.org. You will also find additional internet resources at the end of this book.

INTERNET RESOURCES

Alliance for Care at the End of Life: http://www.afceol.org
American Academy of Hospice and Palliative Medicine:
    http://www.aahpm.org
American Hospice Foundation: http://www.americanhospice.org
Association for Death Education and Counseling:
    http://www.adec.org
Canadian Hospice Palliative Care Association:
    http://www.chpca.net
Caring Connections: http://www.caringinfo.org
Center for Death Education and Bioethics:
    http://www.uwlax.edu/Sociology/cde&b
Center to Advance Palliative Care: http://www.capc.org
Centers for Disease Control and Prevention: http://www.cdc.gov
Cicely Saunders International:
    http://www.cicelysaundersfoundation.org
Compassion and Choices: http://www.compassionandchoices.org
Death Cafe: http://www.deathcafe.com
Hospice and Palliative Nurses Association: http://www.hpna.org
Hospice Association of America: http://www.nahc.org
Hospice Education Institute: http://www.hospiceworld.org
Hospice Foundation of America: http://www.hospicefoundation.org
Hospice Information Service: http://www.hospiceinformation.info

International Association for Hospice and Palliative Care:
http://www.hospicecare.com

Medicare/Medicaid complete listing of state reimbursement
methodologies:
http://kff.org/medicaid/state-indicator/hospice-care/

National Cancer Institute, Cancer Information Service:
http://www.cis.nci.nih.gov

National Hospice Foundation:
http://www.nationalhospicefoundation.org

National Hospice and Palliative Care Organization:
http://www.nhpco.org

National Palliative Care Research Center: http://www.npcrc.org

St. Christopher's Hospice, Sydenham, London:
http://www.stchristophers.org.uk

The Conversation Project: theconversationproject.com

The Institute of Medicine report: *Unequal Treatment: Confronting Racial and Ethnic Disparities in Health Care*

Worldwide Palliative Care Alliance: http://www.thewpca.org

REFERENCES

Chapter 2

1   Starr, P. *The Social Transformation of American Medicine* (Basic Books, 1982), 11, 22, 32, 75, 151, 169.
    Krisman-Scott, M.A. "Origins of Hospice in the United States. The Care of the Dying, 1945-1975." *Journal of Hospice and Palliative Nursing* 5(4) (October-December, 2003): 205-210.
2   Krisman-Scott, M.A. *Origins of Hospice.*
    President's Commission for the Study of Ethical Problems in Medicine and Biomedical and Behavioral Research. *Deciding to Forego Life-Sustaining Treatment* (Washington, DC: US Government Printing Office, 1983).
3   Starr, P. *Social Transformation.*
4   Krisman-Scott, M.A. *Origins of Hospice.*
    Lerner, M. "The dying patient" in Scotch, N. ed. *When, Why and Where People Die.* (New York: Russell Sage Foundation, 1970) 5-29.
5   Krisman-Scott, M.A. *Origins of Hospice.*
    Goldhill, D. *Catastrophic Care. How American Health Care Killed My Father and How We Can Fix It.* (New York: Alfred A. Knopf, Inc., 2013), 26-7, 46, 33-4.
6   Brawley, O.W. *How We Do Harm. A Doctor Breaks Ranks about Being Sick in America.* (New York: St. Martin's Press, 2011), 23, 115, 122-3.
7   Krisman-Scott, M.A. *Origins of Hospice.*
    Starr, P. *Social Transformation.*

8   *National Vital Statistics Report*. Centers for Disease Control and Prevention. 2012 October, 61(6).

9   Munn, J. "Telling the Story: Perceptions of Hospice in Long-Term Care." *American Journal of Hospice and Palliative Medicine* 29(3) (2012): 201-209.

10 Melhado, L. "Exploring Uncertainty in Advance Care Planning in African Americans: Does Low Health Literacy Influence Decision Making Preference at End of Life." *American Journal of Hospice and Palliative Medicine* 28(7) (2011): 495-500.
    Satcher, D., and R.J. Pamies. *Multicultural Medicine and Health Disparities. New York*. (NY: McGraw-Hill Companies, Inc., 2006).

11 Munn, J. "Telling the Story."
    Krisman-Scott, M.A. *Origins of Hospice.*

12 Glass, A.P. and Nahapetyan. "Discussions by Elders and Adult Children about End-of-Life Preparation and Preferences." *Preventing Chronic Disease. Public Health Research, Practice, and Policy* 5(1) (January, 2008): 1-8.
    Minino, A.M., et al. "Deaths: Preliminary Data for 2004." *National Vital Statistics Report* 54(19) (2006): 1-49.
    Teitelbaum, H.S., et al. *The Epidemiology of Hospice and Palliative Care.* (Disease-a-month, 2013, 59), 309-324.
    Krisman-Scott, M.A. *Origins of Hospice.*
    Chronic Disease Prevention and Health Promotion. Centers for Disease Control and Prevention Website, http://www.csc.gov/chronicdisease/overview/indes.html, 2012. Accessed December 2013.

13 Goldhill, D. *Catastrophic Care. How American Health Care Killed My Father and How We Can Fix It.* (New York: Alfred A. Knopf, Inc., 2013), 26-7, 46, 33-4.

14 Melhado, L. "Exploring Uncertainty."
    Teitelbaum, H.S., et al. *Epidemiology.*

15 Browning, A.M. "Empowering Family Members in End-of-Life Care Decision Making in the Intensive Care Unit." *Dimensions of Critical Care Nursing* 28(1) (2008): 18-23.

16   Glass, A.P., and Nahapetyan, L. *Discussions by Elders.*
     Robert Wood Johnson Foundation. *Means to a better end: a report on dying in America today.* (Washington, DC: 2002) http://www.rwjf.org/files/publications/other/meansbetterend.pdf.

17   Gries, C. et al. "Family Member Satisfaction with End-of-Life Decision-making in the Intensive Care Unit." *Chest* 133(3) (March, 2008): 704-712.

18   Goldhill, D. *Catastrophic Care.*
     Glass, A.P., and L. Nahapetyan. *Discussions by Elders.*
     Munn, J. "Telling the Story."
     Miller, S.C., et al. "Hospice Enrollment and Hospitalization of Dying Nursing Home Patients." *The American Journal of Medicine* 111 (July, 2001): 38-44.

Chapter 3

1   *Surrogate Decision Maker.* Wikipedia, 2014. Last revision February 7, 2014. http://en.wikipedia.org/wiki/Surrogate_decision-maker
     Emanuel, L.L., and S.L. Librach. *Palliative Care: Core Skills and Clinical Competencies.* 2nd Edition. (St. Louis, MO: Elsevier Saunders, 2011), 271-2
     Council on Ethical and Judicial Affairs 4-A-01, *Surrogate Decision Making.* Reference Committee on Amendments to Constitution and Bylaws. American Medical Association, 2001.
     Lang, F., and T. Quill. "Making Decisions with Families at the End of Life." *American Family Physician* 70:719723 (2004).
     Wittich, A.R., et al. "'He Got His Last Wishes': Ways of Knowing a Loved One's End-of-Life Preferences and Whether Those Preferences Were Honored." *The Journal of Clinical Ethics* 24(2) (2013): 113-24.

2   Council on Ethical and Judicial Affairs 4-A-01. *Surrogate Decision Making.*

3   *Health Care Surrogates: What do I need to know?* http://www.wvlegalservices.org. Accessed 3/19/2014
     Emanuel, L.L. and S.L. Librach. *Palliative Care.*
     "Surrogate Decision Maker" Wikipedia.

4   Lang, F., and T. Quill. "Making Decisions."
     Medicare.gov. The Official U.S. Government Site for Medicare.
     http://www.medicare.gov/coverage/hospice-and-respite-care.html#.
     Accessed 4/26/2014.
     Wittich, A.R., et al. "'He Got His Last Wishes': Ways of Knowing
     a Loved One's End-of-Life Preferences and Whether Those
     Preferences Were Honored." *The Journal of Clinical Ethics* 24(2)
     (2013): 113-24.
     Council on Ethical and Judicial Affairs 4-A-01. *Surrogate Decision
     Making*
     Swetz, K.M., et al. "Surrogate Decision-Making and the Need
     for Advance Care Planning: Issues raised by the Al Barnes Case."
     Minnesota Medicine, April, 2011. http://www.minnesotamedicine.
     com/tabid/3730. First accessed March 29, 2014
5   Silveira, M.J., et al. "Advance Directives and Outcomes of Surrogate
     Decision Making before Death." *New England Journal of Medicine*
     362(13) (2010): 1211-1218.
6   *"Surrogate Decision Maker"* Wikipedia.

Chapter 4

1   Silveira, M.J., et al. "Advance Directives."
     Omnibus Budget Reconciliation Act of 1990, Public Law No. 101-
     5088, 1990.
     Glass, A. P., and Nahapetyan, L. *Discussions by Elders.*
2   Silveira, M.J., et al. "Advance Directives."
     Omnibus Budget Reconciliation Act of 1990.
     Wittich, A. R. et al. "'He Got His Last Wishes.'"
3   Out-of-Hospital Cardiac Arrest Surveillance—Cardiac Arrest
     Registry to Enhance Survival (CARES), United States, October
     1, 2005—December 31, 2010. Morbidity and Mortality Weekly
     Report (MMWR). http://ww.cdc.gov/mmwr/preview/mmwrhtml/
     ss6008a1.html. Accessed 3/25/2014.

Sasson, C. et al. "Predictors of Survival From Out-of-Hospital Cardiac Arrest: A Systematic Review and Meta-Analysis." *Circulation* 3 (2010): 63-81.

Neagle, J.T., and K. Wachsberg. "What Are the Chances a Hospitalized Patient Will Survive In-Hospital Arrest?" *The Hospitalist* (2010). http://www.the-hospitalist.org/details/article/834467. Accessed 3/25/2014.

[4] Resuscitation Committee, Academic Medical Center, University of Amsterdam, The Netherlands. "In-Hospital Cardiopulmonary Resuscitation: Prearrest Morbidity and Outcome." *Archives of Internal Medicine* 159(8) (1999): 845-850.

Neagle, J.T. and K. Wachsberg. "What Are the Chances …?"

Chapter 5

[1] Wittich, A.R., et al. "'He Got His Last Wishes.'"

Detering, K.M., et al. "The Impact of Advance Care Planning on End of Life Care in Elderly Patients: Randomized Controlled Trial." *British Medical Journal* 340 (2010): c1345.

Emanuel, L.L., and S.L. Librach. *Palliative Care.*

Chapter 6

[1] Pal, S.K., and A. Hurria. "Impact of Age, Sex and Comorbidity on Cancer Therapy and Disease Progression." *Journal of Clinical Oncology* 28(26) (September 10, 2010): 4086-4093.

[2] Emanuel, L.L., and S.L. Librach. *Palliative Care.*

Krisman-Scott, M. A. *Origins of Hospice.*

[3] "The History of Hospice and Palliative Care." *Current Problems in Cancer* 35 (2011): 304-309.

WHO Definition of Palliative Care. World Health Organization, http://www.who.int/cancer/palliative/definition/en/. Accessed December 28, 2013

Emanuel, L.L., and S.L. Librach. *Palliative Care.*

Teitelbaum, H.S., et al. *Epidemiology.*

4   "The History of Hospice and Palliative Care."
      WHO Definition of Palliative Care. World Health Organization,
      http://www.who.int/cancer/palliative/definition/en/.   Accessed
      December 28, 2013
      Emanuel, L.L., and S.L. Librach. *Palliative Care.*
      Teitelbaum, H.S., et al. *Epidemiology.*

Chapter 7

1   Miller, S.C., et al. "Hospice Enrollment."
      Steele, L.L., et al. "The Quality of Life of Hospice Patients: Patient
      and Provider Perceptions." *American Journal of Hospice & Palliative
      Medicine* 22(2) (2005): 95-109;
      Hoffmann, R.L. "The Evolution of Hospice in America: Nursing's
      Role in the Movement." *Journal of Gerontological Nursing* (July
      2005): 26-34.
      "The History of Hospice and Palliative Care."
2   Connor, S.R. *Hospice and Palliative Care, The Essential Guide.* 2nd
      Edition. (New York: Routledge, 2009).
      Forster, T. et al. "Hospice in the United States Expands, Evolves
      over 30 years-A Data Review." *Caring* (April 2013): 18-25.
      Hoffmann, R.L. "The Evolution of Hospice."
      Steele, L.L., et al. "The Quality of Life."
      Teitelbaum, H.S. et al. *Epidemiology.*
      Miller, S.C. et al. "Hospice Enrollment."
      Munn, J.C. "Telling the Story."
      Krismann-Scott, M.A. *Origins of Hospice.*
3   Hoffmann, R.L. "The Evolution of Hospice."
4   Melhado, L. "Exploring Uncertainty."
      Steele, L.L., et al. "The Quality of Life."
      Abba, K., et al. "Interventions to encourage discussion of end-of-
      life preferences between members of the general population and
      the people closest to them—a systematic literature review." *BMC
      Palliative Care* 12(40) (2013): 1-12.

5 Emanuel, L.L. and S.L. Librach. *Palliative Care*, 8.
Connor, S.R. *Hospice and Palliative Care*, 9.

6 Andruccioli, J., et al. "Illness Awareness of Patients in Hospice: Psychological Evaluation and Perception of Family Members and Medical Staff." *Journal of Palliative Medicine* 10(3) (2007): 741-748.

7 Steele, L.L., et al. "The Quality of Life."

8 Hoffmann, R.L. "The Evolution of Hospice."

9 Teitelbaum, H.S., et al. *Epidemiology.*

10 "The History of Hospice and Palliative Care."

11 Connor, S.R. *Hospice and Palliative Care*, 286.

12 "The History of Hospice and Palliative Care."

13 Connor, S.R. *Hospice and Palliative Care.*
Starr, P. *Social Transformation.*

14 "The History of Hospice and Palliative Care."

15 Hoffmann, R.L. "The Evolution of Hospice."
Forster, T., et al. "Hospice in the United States Expands, Evolves over 30 years—A Data Review." *CARING* 32(4) (April, 2013): 18-25;
"The History of Hospice and Palliative Care."
Krisman-Scott, M.A. *Origins of Hospice.*
Neigh, J. "The Evolution of Hospice: From Volunteer Inception to Professional Business." *CARING* 24(11) (November, 2005): 7-14.
Miller, S.C., et al. "Hospice Enrollment."

16 Hoffmann, R.L. "The Evolution of Hospice."
Forster, T., et al. "Hospice in the United States Expands."

17 National Hospice and Palliative Care Organization. *NPHCO's Facts and Figures. Hospice Care in America.* 2013 Edition.
Forster, T., et al. "Hospice in the United States Expands."

18 Forster, T., et al. "Hospice in the United States Expands."

19 Levinson, D.R. Hospice Beneficiaries' Use of Respite Care. Department of Health & Human Services Memorandum Report (Washington, DC: 2008).
Hoffmann, R.L. "The Evolution of Hospice."
Miller, S.C., et al. "Hospice Enrollment."
Medicare.gov. "Hospice and Respite Care."

Teitelbaum, H.S., et al. *Epidemiology.*

Medicare Hospice Benefits. US Department of Health and Human Services Publication. Centers for Medicare and Medicaid Services. CMS Product No. 02154. Revised August 2013.

[20] Forster, T., et al. "Hospice in the United States Expands."
Emanuel, L.L. and S.L. Librach. *Palliative Care,* 604.

[21] Munn, J. "Telling the Story."
Connor, S.R. Hospice and Palliative Care, 133.

[22] Levinson, D.R. Hospice Beneficiaries.

[23] Swetz, K. et al. "Surrogate Decision-Making."
"The History of Hospice and Palliative Care."

[24] Swetz, K. et al. Surrogate Decision-Making.
"The History of Hospice and Palliative Care."
Connor, S.R. *Hospice and Palliative Care,* 126-133.
Medicare Hospice Benefits. U.S. Department of Health & Human Services, Centers for Medicare & Medicaid Services, CMS Product No. 02154. Revised August 2013. Accessed 5/21/2014.

[25] Saraiya, B., et al. "End of Life Planning and its Relevance for Patients and Oncologists' Decisions in Choosing Cancer Therapy." *Cancer* 12 Supplement (December 15, 2009); 3540-3547.
Glass, A.P., and L. Nahapetyan. *Discussions by Elders.*
Saraiya, B., et al. "End of Life Planning."
Moorman, S.M., and M. Inoue. "Persistent Problems in End-of-Life Planning Among Young and Middle-Aged American Couples." *Journal of Gerontology Series B: Psychological Sciences and Social Sciences* 68(1) (2012): 97-106.
Krisman-Scott, M.A. *Origins of Hospice.*
Jenkins, T.M., et al. "Barriers to Hospice Care in Alabama: Provider-Based Perceptions." *American Journal of Hospice & Palliative Medicine* 28(3) (2011): 153-160.
Weissman, D.E. "Decision Making at a Time of Crisis Near the End of Life." *Journal of American Medical Association* 292(14) (October 13, 2004: 1738-1743.
McNeilly, D.P., and K. Hillary. "The Hospice Decision: Psychosocial Facilitators and Barriers." OMEGA 35(2) (1997): 193-217.

Cherlin, E., et al. "Communication between Physicians and Family Caregivers about Care at the End of Life: When Do Discussions Occur and What is Said?" *Journal of Palliative Medicine* 8(6) (December, 2005): 1176-1185.

Dussen, D.V., et al. "Perceptions About Hospice From a Community-Based Pilot Study: Lessons and Findings." *American Journal of Palliative Care* 28(6) (2011): 418-423.

Teitelbaum, H.S., et al. *Epidemiology.*

Emanuel, L.L. and S.L. Librach. *Palliative Care.*

Caralis, P.V., et al. "The Influence of Ethnicity and Race on Attitudes toward Advance Directive, Life-Prolonging treatments, and Euthanasia." *Clinical Ethics* (1993): 268.

Melhado, L. "Exploring Uncertainty."

Rhodes, R.L., et al. "African American Bereaved Family Members' Perceptions of the Quality of Hospice Care: Lessened Disparities, But Opportunities to Improve Remain." *Journal of Pain and Symptom Management* 34(5) (2007): 472-479.

[26] Weissman, D.E. "Decision Making at a Time of Crisis."

[27] National Hospice and Palliative Care Organization.

[28] Teno, J.M., et al. "Timing of Referral to Hospice and Quality of Care: Length of Stay and Bereaved Family Members' Perceptions of the Timing of Hospice Referral." *Journal of Pain and Symptom Management* 34(2) (August, 2007): 120-125.

[29] Teno, J.M., et al. "It is 'Too Late' or is it? Bereaved Family Member Perceptions of Hospice Referral When Their Family Member was on Hospice for Seven Days or Less." *Journal of Pain and Symptom Management* 43(4) (April, 2012): 732-738.

Teno, J.M., et al. "Timing of Referral to Hospice."

Dussen, D.V., et al. "Perceptions about Hospice."

Neigh, J. "The Evolution of Hospice."

[30] National Hospice and Palliative Care Organization.

Dussen, D.V., et al. "Perceptions about Hospice."

Teno, J.M., et al. "It is 'Too Late' or is it?"

[31] "The History of Hospice and Palliative Care."

www.ingramcontent.com/pod-product-compliance
Lightning Source LLC
Chambersburg PA
CBHW050409290526
45786CB00003B/1183